Photography in New Orleans

A priest, *ca.* 1865. *Carte-de-visite* by Charles Marmu.
From the collections of the Louisiana State Museum

Photography in New Orleans

The Early Years, 1840–1865

Margaret Denton Smith and
Mary Louise Tucker

Louisiana State University Press
Baton Rouge and London

Manufactured in the United States of America

Designer: Joanna Hill
Typeface: Galliard
Typesetter: Graphic Composition
Printer: Thomson-Shore, Inc.
Binder: John Dekker and Sons

Library of Congress Cataloging in Publication Data

Smith, Margaret Denton.
Photography in New Orleans.

Bibliography: p.
Includes index.
1. Photography—Louisiana—New Orleans—History.
I. Tucker, Mary Louise. II. Title
TR24.L8S64 770′.9763′35 81–18580
ISBN 0–8071–0987–8 AACR2

For Robert B. Smith and
Thomas W. Tucker

Contents

Illustrations

Acknowledgments

During the course of preparing this book we received extraordinarily generous responses from several individuals and institutions. Special thanks go to Robert R. Macdonald, director, Louisiana State Museum, who gave us access to the museum's large collection of early New Orleans photographs, and to J. B. Harter, curator of paintings and graphic arts at the museum, for his assistance with the materials. Also most helpful were the staffs at the Historic New Orleans Collection, the Special Collections Division of the Howard-Tilton Memorial Library at Tulane University and the Department of Archives and Manuscripts of the Troy H. Middleton Library at Louisiana State University, other major repositories of New Orleans photographs.

Invaluable information was offered by William F. Stapp, curator of photography, National Portrait Gallery; David Haynes, Institute of Texan Cultures, University of Texas at San Antonio; Norton Simon, curator, Pensacola Historical Society; Mrs. Allen Morris, State Photographic Archives, Florida State University, Tallahassee; Les Jensen, curator of collections, Museum of the Confederacy, Richmond; Ann J. Abadie, associate director, Center for the Study of Southern Culture, University of Mississippi; Brandt Rowles, who gave us access to his New Orleans stereographic views, now in the collection of the Louisiana State Museum; and Charles East, who shared his collection of New Orleans materials.

We are indebted to William Welling for his encouragement and especially for his recent book, *Photography in America: The Formative Years, 1839–1900*, which was a source of detailed information, and to Beaumont Newhall, who procured permission for us to publish the view of Canal Street in a German collection. We also wish to thank the editors of *Louisiana History*, in which the Biographical Checklist of New Orleans Photographers first appeared in somewhat different form as "A Checklist of Photographers Working in New Orleans, 1840–1865" (Fall, 1979).

Photography in New Orleans

Introduction

This study discusses the practice of photography in New Orleans from the first exhibitions in 1840 through the years of the Civil War and its aftermath. The early history of photography in the Crescent City was similar to that of many cities in the United States. There was at first a reaction of total amazement to the daguerreotype; local commentators expressed curiosity and delight in the process that enabled one to create pictures with light.

A daguerreotype was a unique image formed upon a silvered copper plate that had been made light-sensitive by exposure to the vapors of various substances such as iodine, bromine, and chlorine. The French-speaking community took particular pride in the fact that the first popular photographic images originated with their countryman, Louis Jacques Mandé Daguerre.

In March, 1840, six months after the public disclosure of the process in Paris, Jules Lion, a portrait painter and lithographer, exhibited the first successful daguerreotype views in New Orleans.[1] In other American cities, artists and scientists had begun experiments in September, 1839, when long-anticipated news of the invention reached the eastern seaboard. With limited information, pioneer photographers such as Samuel F. B. Morse, Joseph Saxton, and Alexander S. Wolcott tried various camera designs and combinations of light-sensitive chemicals. Six months before Lion's exhibitions in New Orleans, Morse and D. W. Seager each exhibited daguerreotype views of New York City. The following month, Saxton exhibited views of Philadelphia. Many of these men were already involved in professions related to optics, chemistry, or metallurgy. They and other early enthusiasts collaborated with doctors, professors, and inventors to produce their views. That Lion, working in relative isolation in New Orleans, was able to produce daguerreotype plates in March of 1840 is especially noteworthy. (It is possible that Lion's brother Achille, a dentist, contributed some expertise to his early experiments.)[2]

Portrait making, rather than landscapes, was the object of the most intense and private experiments by all early photographers. America was recovering from the Panic of 1837, and great business opportunities were anticipated in the production of instantaneous likenesses. Because the earlier daguerreotype methods required three- to five-minute exposures, portraits with the subject's eyes open were at first difficult to make. Finding a means to reduce the exposure time to a matter of seconds was essential. In the early winter of 1839–1840, John Johnson, Wolcott, and Henry Fitz, Jr., all of New York, were experimenting with special light reflectors in a camera of their own design. About the same time, Dr. Paul Beck Goddard of Philadelphia discovered the benefit of sensitizing the undeveloped silver plate with bromine. Goddard collaborated with Robert Cornelius, an inventor and metalworker, who produced a self-portrait in November of 1839.[3] Goddard's approach ultimately proved the most practical and popular method of accelerating the exposure time. Efforts of these men were closely guarded secrets; Wolcott's camera was patented on May 8, 1840, and Goddard's bromine technique was not generally known for another year. Any daguerreotype portraits made in New Orleans in 1840 or 1841 have not been found to date.

In the winter of 1842, a few daguerreotypists from other cities arrived with skills in the art of portrait making. They were but a fraction of thousands of newcomers who came seeking their fortunes in the Crescent City, then the fourth largest city and second busiest port in the nation. Attracted by the business opportunities and the social activities of the winter season, these daguerreotypists were accorded an enthusiastic reception by newspapers and patrons. Several skilled operators, such as William H. Harrington, James

Maguire, Thomas Jefferson Dobyns, and Edward Jacobs, stayed long in the city; scores of itinerants came for a short time and moved on. With only two exceptions, New Orleans' earliest photographers were not native to the area.

A few operators of renown, Marcus A. Root, Ezekiel Hawkins, and John Plumbe, came briefly to the city and influenced local practice. Harrington, Maguire, Dobyns, and John Hawley Clarke were active in their art at the national level and received instruction from important innovators in the field. They were able to offer the new collodion processes—ambrotypes, tintypes, paper photographs, and scores of variations—soon after their introduction in the major photographic centers in the East.

In 1851 Frederick Scott Archer, an Englishman, developed a method of using a light-sensitive collodion emulsion as the medium for creating a negative image. When the negative was formed upon a glass plate and backed by a dark ground, the image appeared positive. This unique photograph was called an *ambrotype*. When the negative was formed on a thin iron sheet, which had been japanned black or dark brown, it was called a *ferrotype* or *tintype*. This was also a unique image. Photographs upon glass or common sheet metal were much cheaper to produce than daguerreotypes, which required more precious metals as well as hours of preparation. But the most important use of the collodion process was for the production of glass negatives from which many paper positives could be made, thus introducing a means of rapid production of inexpensive multiple prints.

Prosperity in New Orleans reached its peak in the 1850s. The popularity of photography created a need for larger establishments with a host of anonymous operators to satisfy the needs of patrons. Several galleries were as elegant as those found in New York or Boston. A few independent portraitists, like Lion, who earlier had added daguerreotyping to their skills as painters or lithographers, could not survive such competition. By the mid-fifties, some found themselves in the employ of the larger firms, coloring the photographic portraits to resemble paintings; others had ceased the practice of photography altogether. Men such as Jacobs, whose only profession was photography, concentrated on producing images of high quality in their sumptuous surroundings.

If New Orleans was like other American cities in its enthusiastic acceptance and participation in the development of the photographic processes the first two decades, it was radically different from them in the 1860s. In 1861 the trend was dramatically reversed by the events and consequences of the Civil War: the blockade of the port, federal occupation and confiscation of property, and finally Reconstruction government. A tragic decline in private fortunes and quality of life persisted for almost twenty years. The hiatus of photography caused by the war marked in many cases the ends of careers that were so prominent earlier—those of Dobyns, Harrington, and then Jacobs.

The war created a shift from an emphasis on leisurely portrait making to a fast turnout of inexpensive images such as the tintype and *carte-de-visite*, which recorded the faces of the young soldiers and their families as well as the generals of opposing armies. The *carte-de-visite* was a small paper photograph, usually 2½ by 4 inches, which was mounted on a card about the size of a visiting card. It was a French invention, patented in 1854. Works of this type were mailed by the thousands to loved ones, who placed them in albums as cherished mementos or popular souvenirs. The war also contributed to the expansion of the photographer's interests and to commissions beyond the portrait. Jay D. Edwards, William D. McPherson and Mr. Oliver, Gustave Moses, and Eugene A. Piffet—all participated in recording a tragic part of their country's history.

After the war New Orleans began the slow process of recovery. Some businesses survived; others had to be restarted. In the photographic field there were still some familiar names—William W. Washburn, Samuel T. Blessing, the Moses family, John H. Clarke—but most of the names were new. Portrait studios were prevalent, but now they were joined by such firms as those of Blessing and Theodore Lilienthal, who published stereographic views of the city. A stereo card consisted of two similar photos, each approximately three inches square, mounted side by side on a card. When viewed through a magnifying lens, the scene appeared three dimensional, to the astonishment of the viewer.

In twenty-five years, photography in New Orleans evolved from a one-man artistic endeavor to a business-oriented profession intent on the rapid production of inexpensive prints. The multiplication character inherent in the paper photographic processes was fully exploited. The stereo view card became as popular an item as the *carte-de-visite*, and in 1866 the cabinet portrait was introduced. This was a print, 4 by 5½ inches, mounted on a card that was 4¼ by 6½ inches. By 1865 the paper photograph had replaced the unique images of the daguerreotype and ambrotype, and the tintype was in declining use.

But the stereo view and the cabinet card are parts of the story of professional photography in the last thirty-five years of the nineteenth century. In 1869 several important changes occurred. A method for retouching the negative rather than the finished print revolutionized the portrait business; the opening of the American West by the railroad companies stimulated an interest in landscape photography and boosted the stereo card trade.[4] In 1871 a radical change was made by a British physician, Richard L. Maddox, who took the first steps in the development of a gelatin-based negative, which would eventually lead to the production of cameras for the millions.[5] Photography was then taken out of the exclusive domain of the professional operator, who offered traditional and formal images, and was put into the hands of the amateur who used the camera for personal expression.

I
The Daguerreotype Arrives in New Orleans

The New Orleans population in 1840 was just over 100,000, a mixture of descendants of the early settlers who came from France, Spain, eastern Europe, and England, as well as from the eastern and midwestern sections of the United States. In the Vieux Carré simple cottages abutted handsomely proportioned houses with iron galleries and classical decorations. The new buildings of the American sector above Canal Street frequently had revival-style elements borrowed from the pattern books of Menard Lafever. Incongruously, these fine buildings were situated on narrow, unimproved streets, some leading from the Mississippi River into the cypress swamps. One contemporary observer described New Orleans as a picturesque city with the appearance of "a provincial town in France, badly paved, badly drained, badly kept," but alive with Gallic gaiety.[1]

The port of New Orleans, terminal for crops and products from the entire Mississippi River Valley, rivaled New York City in volume of trade. The city was steadily recovering from the financial crisis of 1837, which had closed banks and commercial houses all over America. On Christmas Day, 1839, a writer for the New Orleans *Commercial Bulletin* predicted with optimism: "Who cannot look forward to a day when it [New Orleans] will assume the first rank among the cities of the world. It is destined to be the 'queen of nations,' the Venice of the seas, and the emporium of an internat[ional] commerce with whose incalculable magnitude, the richest flood that was ever poured from the valley of the fertile Nile would not compare. The thoroughfare of a valley near three thousand miles square . . . the great receptacle of a growing commerce from abroad; there is no power, physical or political, can impede its gigantic advancement."

A promise of renewed prosperity lured waves of immigrants, many of them laborers, and also professionals, shopkeepers, and entrepreneurs, such as the first photographers. Another writer was obliged to add a note of caution. "Hundreds of strangers are daily arriving in our city. Every ship from the sea, every boat from the interior comes crowded with a host of passengers. They throng our streets and public resorts, imparting to the city the aspect of bustle and business. Thousands come annually in quest of 'situations'—the means of gaining a subsistence by personal labor. But unfortunately for these persons business in New Orleans is not so flourishing as it has been in years past, and in consequence hundreds are doomed to disappointment."[2]

During this era of mass migration New Orleans had the appearance of a frontier town. It was the westernmost gate for thousands of people seeking a future in the American Southwest. This influx included Europeans but was predominately composed of Americans from the upper South and the East. Many moved inland to Texas or Arkansas, but large numbers remained. Conflicts between the conservative Creole community and the expanding American population—differences in temperament, commercial interests, language, and territorial jealousies—had resulted in the division of the city into three municipalities in 1835. The Creoles primarily occupied the First District, the Vieux Carré, which lay between Esplanade Avenue and Canal Street, shown in a view dated 1844–1846 (1). Above Canal was the Faubourg Saint Mary and the Second District, where most of the wealthy Americans had settled. The Third District, below Esplanade, was inhabited primarily by the poorer immigrants: Germans, French, Irish, Spanish, and Americans.

With the arrival of so many, there was a desperate need for a strong centralized government to oversee the port and to deal with civic problems. However, decisions on commercial affairs were often made in favor of vested interests. The city fathers ignored civic responsibilities such as public

1. View of Canal Street, *ca.* 1844–1846. Sixth-plate daguerreotype; operator unknown.
From the collections of the Louisiana State Museum

health and education, while they expended large sums on their own separate empires. One traveler from New York City remarked in his journal that he had never seen the "science of money-making reduced to such perfection." Another charged that the "Crescent City . . . is nothing more or less than a kind of half-way house between civilization and California".[3]

The citizens continually refused taxation, and New Orleans was on the verge of bankruptcy. Without municipal funds little was done for public health and education; nothing was done to improve drainage, which a few enlightened doctors felt was connected with the seasonal recurrence of yellow fever.[4] During this period Louisiana had the largest death rate of any state, and New Orleans of any city. Between 1840 and 1860 approximately fifty thousand people died there of yellow fever. The fever was particularly devastating in 1841, as the *Commercial Bulletin* noted on September 21. "The population is thin indeed compared with what it has been during former epidemic seasons. . . . Had not the great mass of the citizens taken timeous departure and placed themselves beyond the spread of the epidemic . . . the 'doomed city' of New Orleans would have been this season, a *death-spot* on the face of the earth." The wealthy tended to ignore the health problem, for they could flee the city for more favorable climates during the summer.

By the end of the 1840s, the ethnic character of New Orleans had changed. The aggressive merchants and political leaders were more and more frequently from the East and Midwest than from the original Louisiana families. Americans had gained the majority and joined with the Creoles to form the dominant element of the upper class. With the revitalization of the economy there emerged a strong middle class with a voting interest in the future. By 1852 the city government had been reconsolidated.[5]

In a city with changing social structures, where there was a declining influence of the old regime and a formation of new merchant dynasties, the affirmation of the social stature of the family was of considerable importance. Besides fashionable dress, architecture, and furnishings, one of the pleasures and signs of status was having one's portrait made. Since the late eighteenth century New Orleanians had observed the custom of commissioning family portraits. The occasion might commemorate an event or achievement of importance in the life of the subject, such as a betrothal or a military or civic recognition. European and American painters had come finding clients desirous of their services.

To satisfy the loyalties and stylistic inclinations of the French Creole Orleanians, several painters came from Paris during the winter seasons. Some of these were students of the French academies and were polished technicians who produced respectable—and a few remarkable—likenesses. Among them was Louis A. Collas, who worked in New Orleans in the 1820s and also enjoyed a high reputation as miniaturist and portrait painter in Philadelphia and Charleston. Jean-Jacques Vaudechamp worked in New Orleans during the 1840s, earning thousands of dollars each season, according to the reports of William Dunlap, author of the first history of American art.[6] Jacques Amans, the French academician who worked there from 1836 to 1856, painted historical and religious scenes as well as portraits. Other painters who came, such as Theodore Moise and T. T. Fowler, were students of the American masters Gilbert Stuart and Thomas Sully.

A number of naïve painters found ample work in New Orleans. Though most had obtained some degree of schooling, their work retained a directness of observation and description of detail that set them apart. Franz Fleishbein produced the most charming portraits, but he had strong competition from Julien Hudson and Jules Lion, both free men of color, who also had received their training in Paris. Professors of painting and drawing such as Antonio Meucci of Italy and George David Coulon of France painted miniatures and taught the arts to the young ladies and gentlemen of the city to supplement their incomes.

Despite the affluence in the upper ranks of the artistic community, most artists working in the city in the 1840s felt the effects of the recession and were forced to alter their prices accordingly. Thomas J. Jackson, a portrait and miniature painter working in New Orleans in 1841, advertised that "in consequence of the pressure of the times," he would make his prices "much more reasonable than he has done heretofore." Another portrait and miniature painter, Ambrose Andrews, was reported to be doing "a fair business in his line, notwithstanding the times."[7] Indeed the economic situation was not the only threat to these painters, for the early months of 1840 announced the arrival of the daguerreotype in New Orleans. Within the decade the use of the daguerreotype for portrait making significantly affected the livelihood of the portrait artist.

Photography was particularly suited to the taste of the rapidly growing middle class of merchants and professionals in New Orleans at mid-century, for its description of reality and detail gave them what they expected from art. The conventions of traditional oil portraiture were reflected in photography. The subject dressed and posed formally and chose the size and format according to the importance of the occasion and the price he wanted to pay. In the daguerrean era, for example, a whole-plate image of a three-quarter length seated subject was far more costly and ostentatious than the miniature-sized one-sixth plate bust portrait. The whole-plate size, 6½ by 8½ inches, became the standard by which other sizes were measured. Sizes ranged from the one-sixteenth plate, 1⅜ by 1⅝ inches, to the double whole plate, 8½ by 13 inches. Furthermore, several photographic portraits of an individual could be made in a lifetime, whereas only the wealthy patrons commissioned more than one oil portrait. The new medium provided a less costly alternative to oil painting for everyone.

For three hundred years artists and scientists had been searching for a less time-consuming means of reproducing images from nature than the traditional modes of drawing and painting. Since the mid-sixteenth century a *camera obscura* had been used to trace drawings from nature. Numerous attempts to fix the image reflected in the *camera obscura* were made during the eighteenth and nineteenth centuries, but it was not until the 1820s that encouraging results were obtained almost simultaneously by Joseph Nicéphore Niépce and Louis Jacques Mandé Daguerre in France and by William Henry Fox Talbot in England.[8]

Niépce and Daguerre, working independently, were trying to secure a permanent image on metals coated with iodine salts. Niépce is, in fact, credited with making the first photograph, in 1826 on a pewter plate. After he and Daguerre were introduced by their mutual lensmaker Charles Chevalier in 1829, the two inventors pooled their knowledge and formed a partnership. Following the death of Niépce four years later, Daguerre persevered and finally succeeded in securing the image of the *camera obscura* on a silvered copper plate. He announced his discovery in January of 1839, though details of the process were not made public until several months later.

Meanwhile, in England, Talbot by 1835 had moderate success in making small "photogenic drawings" on sensitized paper. He continued with his experiments but probably would have dropped them had it not been for the announcement of Daguerre's discovery. Talbot, jealous of his own idea, hastened to make public his work. On January 31, 1839, Talbot outlined his experiments to the Royal Society, and then on February 21 he gave the group a detailed description of his process.

Talbot's method produced a paper negative from which many inexpensive paper copies could be made. Daguerre's process produced a reversed mirrorlike image on a metal plate that had to be held at a particular angle to be seen properly, without reflection. Furthermore, the daguerreotype was a unique picture. Despite its drawbacks, Daguerre's method was more widely practiced in the first years of the heliographic arts because of its superior image quality and its accessibility through instruction manuals translated into several languages, and because Talbot restricted the use of his process by a patent of 1841. Although Daguerre had taken out a patent for his process in England before the French government gave him an annuity for life and offered his discovery to the world, no such legal restrictions were placed on the use of the daguerreotype in America. The daguerreotype then, rather than the talbotype, dominated photography in America until it was replaced by the collodion processes of the 1850s.

Mention of Daguerre's work appeared everywhere, including America, during the spring and summer of 1839. Samuel F. B. Morse, the American painter and inventor, paid a visit to Daguerre in Paris and wrote a letter to the New York *Observer* describing his impressions of the daguerreotype. "The exquisite minuteness of the delineation cannot be conceived. No painting or engraving ever approached it."[9] The letter was reprinted in newspapers throughout the United States. The public was eager for more news, and other reports followed.

The *United States Magazine and Democratic Review* published a general report comprising excerpts from French and English newspapers. Besides a description of Daguerre's specimens of the new art, the magazine included extracts from a letter by Talbot to the secretary of the Royal Society, communicating his results and how he achieved them.[10]

At a meeting in Paris of the French Academy of Sciences on August 19, 1839, details of Daguerre's process were finally made public. The written accounts of the daguerreotype process reached the United States on September 20 with the arrival in New York of the steam packet *British Queen*, which brought copies of newspapers, including the London *Globe* of August 23. Before the end of September newspapers in Philadelphia, Washington, and Baltimore had published copies of the *Globe* article, and on October 1 the New Orleans *Bee* reprinted it. The English report described the excitement in the crowded hall where François Arago, secretary of the French Academy of Sciences, announced Daguerre's invention and related the method used to make these wonderful images. Though not detailed, these newspaper descriptions of the process were adequate for Americans to attempt to make daguerreotypes.

New Orleans newspapers responded to the public's curiosity with frequent notes and reports about the daguerrean drawings. Before the end of October the *Bee* copied an article from the London *Athenaeum* that briefly described the process and spoke of an inherent problem with the delicate film of mercury on the plate. "One great obstacle to the use of M. Daguerre's photogenic process, is the difficulty of preserving the pictures when completed, because they are of so delicate a nature, and so easily injured, that the slightest touch effaces them—even M. Daguerre himself has always found it necessary to protect them with a plate of glass, which is both inconvenient and troublesome."[11] But the fragility of the plate was only a minor frustration for the New Orleanian who experimented in the late fall and winter of 1839; for either he could import from Paris the costly camera and lens, the chemicals, and plates, or he could make his own equipment and mix his own chemical baths, which was an extremely delicate procedure.

The results of early experiments were at best unpredictable. Even the manuals published by Daguerre, which appeared that autumn, could not substitute for demonstrations and lectures. Daguerre personally trained agents who traveled to various countries. One of them, François Gouraud, came to New York on November 23, 1839, as the representative of the French firm Alphonse Giroux et Compagnie, which published Daguerre's manual and manufactured equipment endorsed by him. Gouraud's job was to establish a market for the daguerreotype in America. He brought about thirty daguerreotypes, supposedly made by Daguerre and his students; to them he added views he had made in New York. The flamboyant ambassador of daguerreotypy invited the gentlemen of the press to his exhibitions. With flattering praise one of them referred to the images as "exquisitely beautiful results of [Daguerre's] wonderful discovery."[12] After two weeks of preliminary publicity, Gouraud opened a public show charging one dollar for admission.

The rage for the daguerreotype in America spread quickly, first along the East Coast, then to the West and South. The New Orleans *Bee* reported on December 27, 1839: "Mr. Gourand [*sic*], of New York, is exhibiting specimens of the Daguerreotype: they are said to be exquisitely beautiful. It is utterly impossible for language to describe their perfections, says the *Commercial Advertiser*, and equally impossible for one who has not seen them to derive from language a just conception of the wonderful effects produced."

Gouraud, well aware of the American public's interest, wrote a letter to the editor of the New York *Evening Post*, which appeared in the January 7, 1840, issue. "As I am in daily receipt of letters from different cities in the Union, requesting me to come and exhibit the proofs and mode of Mr. Daguerre's process, permit me to make use of your columns to reply to all, that I defer to their requests; and that after completing my practical lectures this week, I shall proceed to Philadelphia, Baltimore, Washington, and Charleston, to be in the spring in New Orleans, from whence I go to Havana, before returning to New York, to attend to the improvement of the numerous pupils I hope to leave behind me."

The New Orleans *Bee*, in response to Gouraud's publicized letter, informed the citizens of New Orleans that they would "soon have an opportunity of beholding the wonders of this new and beautiful discovery." However, Gouraud did not come to New Orleans as promised, but rather stayed in New York and New England. When he finally did tour the country, it was to give lectures on his memory system, not the daguerreotype.[13]

One observer, George Vail, who in the early spring of 1840 had completed a tour through the South, wrote Samuel F. B. Morse: "Few if any experiments have been made there. Where they have been it has been done by some scientific gent who attacked it as a matter of curiosity with crude instruments." Vail, on March 11, 1840, had recently returned from New Orleans. Had he remained there a few days longer, he would have had the opportunity of seeing the exhibition of daguerreotypes made not by a "scientific gent" but by an artist.[14]

On March 15, 1840, Jules Lion, the black painter and lithographer, exhibited views "of objects familiar to the residents of New-Orleans, such as the St. Louis Hotel, the Cathedral, the Levee, and a number of public edifices."[15] Lion's first exhibition was held in the hall of the Saint Charles Museum, opposite the Saint Charles Hotel, a popular Sunday gathering place in the American District. He charged one dollar for admission and made a daguerreotype during the exhibition, which was then put up for lottery.

This occasion, like Gouraud's exhibitions in New York City, had been anticipated by editorial fanfare. On March

10, the *Bee* exclaimed: "One will be able to judge by [Lion's work] that the praises of the newspapers are not exaggerated and that Daguerre's process is not below its renown." And *Le Courrier de la Louisiane* of the same day reported that Lion had bettered his competition. "Here, many amateurs have received Daguerreotypes [plates] but either because of impatience, or imperfect knowledge of the precision which is demanded in the use of this instrument, they have again succeeded in obtaining only partially successful prints."

A commentator for the *Bee*, having had his first glimpse of the daguerreotypes, was astonished. "Nothing can be more truly beautiful—The minutest object in the original is reproduced in the copy, and with the aid of a microscope, in a drawing of a few inches square, representing a building some sixty or seventy feet high, the inscriptions on the signs, the divisions between the bricks, the very insect that may have been found upon the wall at the time the impression was taken, are rendered visible. It is a wonderful discovery—one, too, that will prove as useful, as it is admirable."[16] The attention given Lion by the white community at the time when the majority of black people were in slavery is an interesting footnote to the story of this exhibition. Lion had chosen to live and work in a city where attitudes were by no means typical of other cities in the South. As a free man of color, Lion enjoyed a special status, a degree of freedom not accorded to slaves. Most of his caste were skilled artisans and tradesmen, valued members of the commercial and artistic community.

According to the 1850 census of New Orleans, Lion was born in France. In 1831, 1833, 1834, and 1836 he exhibited lithographs at the Paris Salon.[17] In 1837 he arrived in New Orleans where he established a studio in the Vieux Carré. Lion's first subjects were among the most distinguished residents of the city: clergymen, judges, attorneys, and members of the military.[18]

As was the custom with most New Orleans artists, Lion left the city during the hot, humid summers, and in August of 1839 he had the fortune to be in Paris. He may have attended one of Daguerre's early demonstrations there; he may also have acquired equipment manufactured by Daguerre's agent Alphonse Giroux. According to the recollections of another artist, George David Coulon, Lion "brought from France the first Daguerreotype Instrument [to New Orleans]."[19] Lion advertised on September 27, 1839, in the *Bee* that he was once again ready to "resume his profession." The announcement did not mention daguerreotyping, only portrait making.

During that fall and winter a rivalry developed between Lion and another Frenchman, J. B. Pointel du Portail, who also aspired to be the premier daguerrean in the city. A lively competition must have existed between the two. Pointel, also a portraitist and lithographer, had come to New Orleans only the year before Lion. He was the lithographic artist for the *Bee* in 1837, when Lion arrived in the city and met with immediate success. That the first two daguerreotypists advertising in the city were both lithographers suggests that they, like Daguerre, were looking for a method of securing a perfect study that could then be copied in order to make multiple prints. Pointel announced, from February 11 through 13, 1840, in the *Bee* his intention of exhibiting views of the city and harbor of New Orleans as soon as a convenient spot could be selected. But he did not obtain a place to deliver his lecture on the daguerreotype process and exhibit his New Orleans views until April 9. Pointel received no editorial response from the local newspapers, if in fact he did exhibit successful daguerreotypes. On May 2 he advertised his intentions to exhibit his daguerreotypes in Baton Rouge.[20]

By April 9, Lion had already given at least four presentations, including a demonstration at a Creole spring festival, Grand Fête Champêtre, held at the Louisiana Tivoli, a recreation park in a French section of the city. The festivities included fireworks, dinner, and dancing. One correspondent remarked: "I had been prepared to expect something wonderful, but never had anything in my life caused me so much astonishment, as to find nature so closely delineated and copied by means of human invention. This imperishable discovery which gives an existence to shadows and which has revealed an unknown law of nature, merits the attention of every lover of the marvelous and the Philosopher."[21] The magic art became a curiosity and amusement for the gentle class, especially the French, who acknowledged a proprietary interest in their countryman Lion in their journals *L'Abeille de la Nouvelle-Orléans* [the *Bee*] and *Le Courrier.* With every exhibition Lion was encouraged by the newspapers. The *Bee* recommended attendance at the third exhibition, held at the Orleans Ballroom, "with great pleasure, because it is especially intended for the ladies."[22]

At every session, a daguerreotype view was made and then awarded by lottery. As far as it is known, none of Lion's views has survived. However, an 1842 lithograph, *The Cathedral, New Orleans*, has the unmistakable precision of detail, tone, and rendition of perspective that is characteristic of the daguerreotype, and was almost certainly made from a view similar to the one of the cathedral which Lion exhibited in March, 1840 (2).

Presumably, Lion exhibited only views in 1840; several operators in the East, however, were making portraits at that time. Alexander Wolcott and John Johnson opened the first commercially successful portrait studio in New York City in March. Instead of using the apparatus suggested by Daguerre, they employed their own camera, which used a concave, specially ground mirror rather than a lens to concentrate light upon the plate. On March 26, the *Bee* reported Wolcott's having obtained a portrait "of a perfect resemblance." His camera received the first American photography patent in May of 1840. Samuel F. B. Morse also operated a studio in New York with John W. Draper. In Philadelphia Robert Cornelius opened a studio in the summer of 1840 with a silent partner, Dr. Paul B. Goddard, who had found that exposing the daguerreotype plate to bromine rendered it more sensitive to light, thereby decreasing the exposure time. Other portrait makers were Albert S. Southworth, a student of Gouraud, and Joseph Pennell, a student of Morse, who worked in September of that year in a small town just outside of Boston, and John Plumbe, Jr., who worked in Boston and who was to establish a chain of

2. The cathedral, New Orleans, 1842. Lithograph by Jules Lion.
Historic New Orleans Collection

studios in a dozen American cities, including New Orleans.[23]

Although there is no evidence to show that Lion was attempting portraits as well as outdoor views in 1840 or 1841, it seems reasonable to assume that he was. No doubt others in New Orleans, Pointel among them, were also experimenting with portraits—with what results we can only imagine, for no specimens from this period have been found. D. G. Johnson, perhaps the portrait painter and engraver David G. Johnson, was one of those who did experiment with making portraits in New Orleans late in 1840, but he was having difficulties primarily because, he said, of the inferior quality of his materials. In a whining letter to Morse, from whom he had received instruction in the daguerreotype art, he poured forth a litany of complaints.

> I have made some trials . . . and find everything pretty well except the most *important* part, which is the Lenses. . . . The great difficulty is that the Lenses form an imperfect image in *any* position and I have tried them in all and find that they form the best with both convex lenses towards the siter [*sic*] thus [drawing of a man in profile]. I first observed a fullness in the faces I had taken, it making a thin face more fleshy than nature. . . . The Plates I had of Corduan are more or less full of imperfections from flourishing in dust and some of them [are] very bad. The Blue Glass you let me have is very full of vanes and spots, and the cotton I find here is much filled with specks of foreign matter so you see I am in some trouble every way having everything imperfect.

Also, Johnson suggested that his training could have been more thorough or at least longer. "I had so little practice with you that I have to *feel my way* and use my judgement in most things."[24]

If any other operators had been tempted to come to New Orleans in 1841 to make portraits, they would have been dissuaded by news of the devastating yellow fever epidemic of the late summer and early fall. The *Bee* of September 16 observed: "What a remarkable contrast does the city present in a business point of view to the same period last year! Then we were in the full tide of affairs. Now all is stagnant and motionless. The Levee looks deserted; the stores are vacant; few persons appear in our most frequented thoroughfares. Disease appears to have paralyzed our energies." But the newspapers also indicated the general public's continued interest in the art of daguerreotypy. In *L'Abeille*, George Liemne, an importer of French goods, offered "For Sale, a complete daguerreotype, with plates and appendages. The manner in which it may be successfully used will be taught."[25] Innovations were reported as well. "An improvement has recently been made in the Daguerrotype [*sic*], by which the portraits of persons can be taken in a *diffused light*, in from five to fifteen seconds; so that the operator can take the likeness in any weather."[26] In a later article the *Bee* was more specific, "Daguerre has nearly perfected his valuable discovery, in obtaining *instantaneous* impressions by means of electricity. A slight haze, however, is left on the impression, which he wishes to correct before he exhibits the results of his new process. . . . Photography is admirable, but, as to portraits, it is still far from the *whole* truth—the flesh-and-blood reality of the pencil."[27]

In 1839 Daguerre himself was cautious about the practicality of his apparatus for the execution of portraits; two years later he was still trying to resolve difficulties, particularly with the haze or fogging that clouded the plate, with his new galvanizing technique and with the use of bromine accelerators. There were successes among a few operators in the East, but portrait photography was still in an experimental stage.

II
Establishment of Daguerreotype Portrait Galleries

The earliest documented portrait daguerreotype made in New Orleans is that of Judge Alfred Jefferson Lewis, who died there October 24, 1842 (3). The daguerreotypist remains unknown, but he was surely among those operators who first advertised portraits during the winter season of 1841–1842. The yellow fever epidemic of the previous autumn had subsided, and several enterprising daguerreans came to New Orleans to compete for the attention of an eager public. C. Brown and Company and W. B. Foster were apparently in New Orleans by December, for they were listed as daguerreotype operators in an 1842 city directory. Brown advertised on January 26, "Daguerreotype Miniature Portraits [taken] . . . in a superior style . . . at a moderate price. . . . A few seconds' sitting will be sufficient in clear weather."[1] Not to be outdone, Foster claimed to execute daguerreotypes "in a style superior to any heretofore seen in this city," made with a newly acquired instrument from the Parisian optician Noël M. P. Lerebours and manufactured under the supervision of M. Daguerre. One local paper agreed with Foster's assessment of his work, calling his daguerreotypes "some of the finest specimens yet exhibited." Furthermore, Foster enticed his potential patrons with a bargain, "Family groups taken upon a single plate," and invited them to "witness the operation."[2]

The *Daily Picayune* of January 28 announced that James Maguire had opened his rooms on Canal Street for the taking of likenesses. Maguire, a native of Belfast, Ireland, remained in New Orleans for several months, reaping editorial praise for "the finest Daguerreotype likenesses ever seen

3. Judge Alfred Jefferson Lewis, *ca.* 1842. Sixth-plate daguerreotype; operator unknown.
From the collections of the Louisiana State Museum

in the city . . . of startling accuracy and distinctness." Upon his arrival, he had stated his ideas of what a daguerreotype should be, in an advertisement.

> The wonderful fidelity of likenesses taken by this process, can only be conceived by those who have witnessed its re-

> sults. For beauty and delicacy of delineation, and for forcible and lifelike expression no other can compare with the Daguerreotype—the picture presents a counter part of the original so perfect, that it cannot possibly be mistaken. A portrait is of value only so far as it exhibits a true resemblance of the object. Nor is a mere resemblance in drawing sufficient, unless at the same time the living *expression* of the original is preserved. In these particulars, the Daguerreotype is beyond praise—It is truth itself. There is a reason for this. It is, that the picture is not the work of man's hand. Its fidelity depends not on the accuracy of a human eye, or the skillful guidance of an artist's pencil. The delineation is made in a manner which yet remains a mystery, through the sole agency of the subtle medium of light. It is an image optically perfect, which *impresses itself* upon a surface of silver properly prepared to receive it. In all cases, therefore, the resemblance may be confidently warranted to prove exact.[3]

Maguire summarized the fascination the daguerreotype held for Americans. Accuracy and realism, a perfect resemblance, were most desired in any art—portraiture or landscape. And the daguerreotype was most suitable to recording likenesses with precision and tonal fidelity. With daguerreotypes, the mechanics of picture making was out of human hands, or so the layman supposed, and the result of activity somewhere between necromancy and alchemy.

In the latter part of May, Maguire departed on a journey up the Mississippi River, including stops in Natchez, Vicksburg, Plaquemine, and Baton Rouge, where he was hailed as "one of the best, if not the very best Daguerreotype artist in the United States." Maguire had received instructions concerning the daguerreotype in Tuscaloosa, Alabama, from Dr. William H. Harrington and Frederick A. P. Barnard, both mathematics professors. Harrington was an early faculty member of LaGrange College, and Barnard taught at the University of Alabama. Barnard began experimenting early with the daguerreotype after reading descriptions given in the New York *Observer*, but conceded in a letter to Samuel Morse that he could not "operate with any great *certainty* of success" and asked for instruction in exchange for a fee and the promise not to divulge the information without Morse's permission. Barnard thought, however, that it would be necessary to tell his assistant, "a gentleman of this place." That this gentleman was Harrington is corroborated by Barnard's letter of July 1, 1841, published in the *American Journal of Science and Arts*. In it he names Harrington as his associate with whom he had been experimenting for about a year with chlorine in an attempt to render the surface of the daguerreotype plate more sensitive to light. According to Barnard they succeeded, "producing a surface so exquisitely sensitive to the action of light, that the image of an illuminated object was formed upon it in the camera in a space of time almost inappreciable."[4]

In October, 1841, when the article appeared, Barnard and Harrington opened a daguerreotype business in Tuscaloosa, exhibiting "specimens of Landscapes, Views and Miniature portraits from the life."[5] In February, 1842, Harrington was in New Orleans and advertised "his rooms for the reception of visitors at the house of Mrs. Page [a boarding establishment]," inviting "the ladies and gentlemen of New Orleans to examine his specimens of miniature portraits after nature." In May, 1842, Harrington moved his studio from Canal Street to Camp Street, but presumably he left New Orleans by midsummer to avoid the seasonal epidemics, and by September was back in Tuscaloosa in business for himself.[6]

During the spring of 1842, others practiced their daguerreotyping skills in the Crescent City. In March, Justus E. Moore opened his rooms in a boardinghouse, Madame Berniaud's, at the corner of Canal Street. Appealing to local sentiment, Moore advertised with a testimonial to his abilities from Andrew Jackson, hero of the Battle of New Orleans. According to Jackson's letter, Moore, one of the first to photograph him in retirement, had solicited the testimonial. Moore offered for sale likenesses of the general, which he had made the previous year at the Hermitage.[7]

In June, one Mr. Honfleur advertised in the amusements section of the newspaper, but with a warning that he would take daguerreotype portraits for only a limited period before returning to his profession as a "Draftsman and Teacher of

Drawing," and a declaration that he intended to sell his "Daguerreotyper with instructions for its use." Many like Honfleur dropped the daguerreotype business as easily as they picked it up. Indeed, early operators were drawn to the new business in the aftermath of the Panic of 1837, for the trade required little capital. Numerous advertisements for equipment appeared, including the following: "A SPLENDID DAGUERREOTYPE APPARATUS FOR SALE. This is a favorable opportunity for a young man, with a small sum of money, to embark in a business which yields a great profit, or for a gentleman of leisure to get a superior apparatus for his own amusement, as it will be sold very low. Complete instructions in the use of the instrument will be given, if desired, without extra charge."[8] Unfortunately, it was because of these hastily trained people of poor talents that many daguerreotypes of the early period were of a very inferior quality. The majority of the early daguerreotypists were not artistically trained. They were interested in daguerreotypy more as a sideline to their regular business than as a sole profession.

Jules Lion, on the other hand, successfully added daguerreotyping to his artistic practice and during the early 1840s introduced several fashions in the art. He advertised "portraits painted or lithographed and daguerreotypes at very moderate prices"; but he also catered to rich clients by offering daguerreotypes "d'un pied de grandeur"—on double whole plates (8½ by 13 inches) that he imported from Paris. The larger plate was only one of his innovations; he also offered "Copies of family pictures, miniatures daguerreotyped for rings and breast pins."[9] Portrait brooches like the one pictured (4) became fashions that replaced the hand-painted miniature portrait jewelry of an earlier era. Lion again usurped the place of the painter when he announced that he would "take portraits of sick or deceased persons if required," in the *Bee* of December 12, 1842. The daguerreotype mementos were treasured all the more because of the nineteenth century's concern with mortality. Keepsake portraits of young children were taken because the infant mor-

4. Alexander S. Norwood of East Feliciana Parish, *ca.* 1855–1860. Brooch; daguerreotypist unknown.
Courtesy of Charles East

tality rate was so high (5 and 6). Some daguerreotypes were even set into gravestones.[10]

Though the solemn aspect of the trade was sometimes required, most daguerreotypes, like oil or pastel portraits, were made to commemorate a special event in the subject's life, such as the achievement of social or financial success, enlistment in the army, or courtship and marriage. One operator recalled that Monday was usually his best day for business. "We attributed this to the Sunday night courtship,

5. Mourning portrait of a young boy, *ca.* 1842–1845. Sixth-plate daguerreotype; operator unknown.
From the collections of the Louisiana State Museum

6. Mourning portrait of a young girl, *ca.* 1842–1845. Sixth-plate daguerreotype; operator unknown.
From the collections of the Louisiana State Museum

when the young couples would agree to exchange daguerreotypes; Monday was sure to bring them."[11]

Conventions of having one's portrait made—formality in pose and appropriateness of dress—were observed, no matter what medium was chosen. The following bit of instruction for sitters appeared in *Godey's Lady's Book*: "In order to obtain a good picture . . . it is also necessary to dress in colors that do not reflect too much light. For a lady, a good dress is of some dark or figured material. White, pink or light blue must be avoided. Lace work, or a scarf or shawl sometimes adds much to the beauty of a picture. A gentleman should wear a dark vest and cravat. For children, a plaid or dark-striped or figured dress is preferred by most Daguerreotypists. Light dresses are in all cases to be avoided."[12]

Properly attired, the sitter was then required to remain absolutely still throughout the exposure time of several seconds. To prevent movement, the operator provided a headrest, usually a semicircle of iron fitted to the back of a chair. For full-length portraits, the subject was required to brace himself against a tall iron support. Among other precautions taken against movement was not posing the hands on the chest, because the motion of breathing disturbed them, resulting in the hands having a thick and clumsy appearance. Quite naturally, the headrests and the concentration on immobility often resulted in a stiffness of pose and expression.

Eliza Ripley, a young lady of New Orleans, recalled that "the artist applied to father [Judge Richard Henry Chinn], as he needed pictures of well-known men for his show-case. His head had been steadied straight in a most unnatural position, with a kind of callipers or steel braces, and he must have been told to 'look up and smile' for a full minute." Posing for the photographer was altogether different from sitting for an oil painting or pastel sketch. It was sometimes compared with another unpleasantness. "Doubtless sitting is a very painful operation. The daguerreotypist has abridged it, as dentists have tooth-drawing; but still very few persons can sit properly, even to an instrument." Many persons were dissatisfied with their portraits when completed, usually because the results were too accurate. As the *Daguerreian Journal* warned, "If you want a good picture, don't let your looks trouble you, for it will surely show in the Daguerreotype. The camera reports Nature's truths."[13]

Clara Solomon, writing in her diary in New Orleans, evidently did not heed the *Journal*'s advice.

> I dislike to have my picture taken to send away, particularly to a place where it will be seen by so many. Oh! on such occasions is my desire to be handsome, more earnest if possible. How gratifying would it be, for as each person to whom it was shown to involuntarily exclaim, 'How beautiful a face!' Well, he [the daguerreotypist] showed them to us, and they were perfect, A.'s & F.'s & S.'s, and they said mine, but I was not satisfied with mine, and complained to Ma that it was not *pretty*. 'Well,' she said, 'did you expect to make a pretty picture? Do ugly people generally?' Wasn't that cruel?[14]

Sometimes the sitter, in preparation for his daguerreotype session, would contrive to project a certain self-conscious image of himself. The favorite of these images was that of the literary man, shown with books surrounding him or his fingers caught between the leaves of a volume.

Most daguerreotypists stressed the natural character of the sitter and used simple settings, concentrating on the sitter rather than on the background. This predilection for simplicity was a particular characteristic of the American attitude toward an appropriate portrait style. It reflected the earlier artistic traditions of American portraitists, particularly the limners, whose simple compositions and distinct outlines resemble those of American daguerreotypes.

In part, this austere composition and arrangement of subject was due to the necessity of concentrating all available light on the subject. From the notes of George Smith Cook (7), a daguerreotypist who worked briefly in New Orleans, one learns of the difficulties encountered.

> Light, The Effect—Dec. 1845.
> Getting proper effect of light is one of the most important objects in taking Pictures, the light should be concentrated

7. George Cook Smith, *ca.* 1843–1845. Copy (*ca.* 1900) of the daguerreotype attributed to a New Orleans operator.
Valentine Museum, Richmond, Va.

> on the sitter as much as possible, having the light to fall equally upon the sitter in all parts, as much as possible, or the Picture will be too much shaded in parts & burnt in others, turn the eye from the greatest light or it will destroy the sight/ the window should not be over 1½ feet from the floor if possible use a light or window for the background alone, using a curtain to produce the right effect. A yellow background of ochre put in with a little [illegible] and put on the white washing. The Camera should be a little elevated above the sitter's face, it softens the features, a ¾ view makes the strongest likeness, but not always the handsomest, for a dark dress turn the sitter's body to the light, & the face away, forward. A light dress, the reverse.[15]

The sitter had a choice of standard plate sizes, ranging from 1⅜ by 1⅝ inches to 6½ by 8½ inches. The most common size was on the one-sixth plate that measured 2¾ by 3¼ inches. In 1840, the Frenchman Hippolyte-Louis Fizeau introduced a method of toning the plate with a solution of gold chloride. In Europe and America, gilding, as the process was called, was immediately adopted for its beauty and practicality. It not only produced warm tones in the picture, but it also gave the surface of the plate greater durability. After the portrait was processed and gilded, it was mounted, covered with a sheet of glass for protection, sealed around the edges and back with paper, fitted with a gilded paper mat or pinchbeck border, and inserted in a case or frame. The daguerreotype cases were borrowed from those made for miniatures and the price one paid for his likeness varied according to the price of the case he chose. Cases were usually made of wood, bound in leather, a leather substitute, or papier-mâché, and lined with silk, velvet, or plush.

Some purists preferred the beauty of the finely developed straight image, with its clear lights and shadows and the lively tone produced by gilding. However, most people preferred colored daguerreotypes, as they were more lifelike and resembled more closely traditional painting. General Jackson had praised the work of Moore with only one reservation: "Nothing wanting but the colors."[16]

By May, 1843, Lion had produced colored daguerreotypes that *L'Abeille* described as "remarkably well executed" and "giving a kind of life" to the portraits. Lion's success was remarkably early, for tinting techniques were still in experimental stages; an article concerning Antoine François Jean Claudet, the eminent French artist and daguerreotypist, and his method of coloring daguerreotypes had only recently appeared in *Le Courrier*. Other local daguerreans, especially James Maguire, were experimenting with color. In April, Maguire was advertising color in Baton Rouge. However, Lion claimed on November 24, 1843, in *L'Abeille* that one could obtain colored portraits in New Orleans only at his rooms. The following year, Lion's daguerreotyping activity subsided, and he returned to painting and lithography as his main profession.[17]

Daguerreans experimented with various methods of tinting plates to satisfy the customers. Between 1840 and 1846, five patents were issued for coloring processes. The simplest way to color the daguerreotype was to use a dry pigment after the gilded plate had been coated with isinglass or some other gum solution. The pigment was stippled onto the plate with a small camel's hair brush. Since Lion was primarily a painter, he was probably hand coloring the daguerreotypes, using this method.

If the daguerreotypist did not have the talent to color his own portraits, he frequently employed a miniaturist to perform the exacting work. In fact, the coloring of daguerreotypes sometimes became the occupation of miniature and portrait painters in New Orleans, for the art of miniature painting came to an almost abrupt halt with the popular adoption of the new art. From 1840 to 1860 daguerreotypists in America produced more portraits than did painters. Americans totally accepted this new style because they could have portraits heretofore unobtainable except by the upper classes. And though the industry was centered in the larger eastern cities, daguerreotypists were working in almost every sizable city.

Between 1840 and 1845, there were perhaps dozens of persons practicing daguerreotypy in New Orleans. In addition to Lion, Pointel, C. Brown and Company, Foster, Maguire, Harrington, Moore, and Honfleur, there were Auguste Dubar, G. Barry, William H. Hutchings, Mr. Chase, Mr. Ely, Edward Jacobs, Marcus Aurelius Root, George Smith Cook, and Charles Nystrand. Christian Mayr, a "portrait, genre painter, designer, daguerreotypist," visited New Orleans in 1844, but according to the local newspapers, only in the capacity of a portrait painter.[18] Many itinerants never advertised in the directories or newspapers; countless New Orleanians were probably photographed by operators who may have visited the city only briefly (8 and 9). Only one of those mentioned, Hutchings, was a native of Louisiana. Lion was French, Maguire was Irish, and Jacobs was English. Ely came from New York, Root and Harrington from Pennsylvania, and Cook from Connecticut.

Root, the famous Philadelphia daguerrean, wrote in his book, *The Camera and the Pencil*, that he had come in 1844 "from Mobile . . . to New Orleans, where, for some time, I paid attention to the art." Early that year Ely also came to the Crescent City and advertised his gallery on Exchange Place, offering instruction in daguerreotyping and apparatus for sale, as well as portrait taking. It was probably he who first instructed George Smith Cook, a painter, in the art. According to the *Photographic Art-Journal*, Cook took over the operations of Ely's gallery. Wishing to combine his daguerreotype gallery with a gallery of paintings, "he entered into a negotiation for Mr. Cook's celebrated gallery of paintings then established in New Orleans." Another George Cooke had opened a "National Gallery of Painting" there in 1844; he died in the city in 1849. George Smith Cook left New Orleans in the summer of 1845, taking cameras, chemicals, and darkroom equipment with him. He headed inland, visiting towns throughout the South for the next four years. According to the *Photographic Art-Journal*, he established galleries in five states before settling in Charleston in 1849.[19]

Of all the operators working in New Orleans during the early 1840s, Jacobs, Harrington, and Maguire were the most popular, with the press at least. In the summer of

8. Nurse with child, *ca.* 1845–1850. Sixth-plate daguerreotype; operator unknown.
From the collections of the Louisiana State Museum

1844, Edward Jacobs opened his gallery at the corner of Camp and Canal streets. He offered "Daguerreotype portraits, true to life, and executed in a splendid style." He was also prepared to instruct students and to sell instruments.[20] Harrington, who reestablished his New Orleans gallery in 1848, and Jacobs both sustained popularity through the decade, but it was Maguire who dominated the competition. Maguire advertised frequently, thus gaining favor of the editors. In addition, he also won several competitions.

9. Monsieur St. Avid, *ca.* 1845–1850. Sixth-plate daguerreotype; operator unknown.
From the collections of the Louisiana State Museum

A showplace for Maguire's work, one that helped him to establish his reputation in the city, was the annual fair of the Agricultural and Mechanics' Association of the State of Louisiana, which was primarily a showcase for mechanical apparatus and agricultural products. The association held its first fair in Baton Rouge in November, 1841; in 1843 a category was created for the judging of daguerreotypes. Prospect of competition spurred local photographers to improve their art. However, Maguire was a consistent winner, and in January of 1843, at the second annual fair, he was awarded a First Premium for his daguerreotypes. The Fine Arts Committee returned their verdict: "Jas. McGuire [*sic*] of New Orleans exhibited a frame containing several superior specimens of miniatures. Mr. McGuire has made the department of portraiture his own in the South by defying competition." The next year Maguire took the First Premium honor once again for the four daguerreotypes he exhibited—two portraits from life and two copies from pictures. This time his entries were in color.[21]

Having established himself in New Orleans, Maguire then traveled to Europe in the summer of 1844 to acquaint himself with the latest improvements. Maguire, no doubt, felt that he had much to gain by going to Paris, where announcements were frequently made by Daguerre and his colleagues concerning the use of new chemicals and equipment. Before departing New Orleans in May, he offered local citizens the opportunity to have their portraits taken and then delivered to relatives in Paris, Vienna, London, Liverpool, Glasgow, Dublin, or Belfast. Not only did he promise to deliver them in person, but he also offered to make daguerreotype portraits of the European relatives for delivery upon his return.[22]

During his absence, Maguire entrusted the operation of his studio to his "ablest and most accomplished pupil," William H. Hutchings. Hutchings kept Maguire's studio open for business during the summer, an unusual effort for a New Orleans artist. Maguire stated, "By every steamer it is my intention to transmit to Mr. Hutchings all the most modern instruments and materials in the Daguerreotype from Paris."[23]

Maguire announced his return in November, 1844, with unabashed self-confidence and enthusiasm in his renewed ability to satisfy every order. He flattered himself "that his previous reputation has not suffered by his diligent and critical visits to the most celebrated Photographers in England and France." Maguire returned with a new method of preparing plates. Daguerre had announced in May a process for coating the plates that allowed the operator to store them for a time before use instead of having to prepare each one as needed. The varnish applied to the plates also increased their sensitivity.[24] Maguire was now ready to take orders in his elegant, refurbished rooms at the corner of Camp and Canal streets. He was also prepared to give instructions in the art, providing all materials needed.

Immediately upon Maguire's return, Hutchings established his own gallery across Canal Street, at the corner of Chartres Street. He advertised in the same paper that announced Maguire's return that he had, "at great expense," made new discoveries and received from Europe and northern cities all the recent improvements in instruments and chemicals. Hutchings' own claim seems to suggest that he and Maguire had fallen out over financial matters or professional jealousies.

It was a bitter exchange the following July when Hutchings, in partnership with H. Whittemore in the Orleans Gallery, received the First Premium at the state fair for daguerreotypes and colored daguerreotypes, while Maguire received the Second Premium.[25] Maguire challenged the decision of the judges in the New Orleans *Daily Tropic*. "James Maguire is ready to stake the sum of one hundred dollars that he can exhibit specimens of the Daguerreotype on a small plate, and five hundred dollars on a large plate, which, by the judgement of a majority in a community of five artists or connoisseurs of this city, shall be pronounced superior to those shown by any other person." Hutchings and Whittemore answered that by the decision of the judges they considered the matter settled. "And as we are not gamblers, but depend upon 'merit' alone for success, we, hereby appoint the 'Public' the Judges of our works." With sharp wits and pens, the battle was waged in the *Daily Tropic* for three weeks. It ended abruptly with a final newspaper notice by Maguire that included an endorsement written by Thomas Bangs Thorpe, one of two judges at the state fair. "With due deference to the gentlemen who composed the Committee of Award . . . we would state our opinion that a Committee of Artists skilled in such matters, should have decided in favor of the Maguire specimens."[26] Thorpe, who was then living in Baton Rouge, would shortly make a name for himself as a humorist, writing for national publications.

By the mid-1840s technical knowledge had improved domestic production of daguerreotyping equipment. Several companies, especially in New York, Boston, and Philadelphia, began specializing in the production of photographic supplies, which led to more efficient and economical business management and, hence, lower prices. Increased competition between manufacturers and suppliers caused a reduction in the price of American-made plates; for example, Scovill Company, of Waterbury, Connecticut, was able to price their plates at $3.50 per dozen in 1845, one-half the price in 1841.[27]

The most important innovation was the introduction of the Petzval portrait lens, manufactured by Voigtländer in Vienna. This lens, introduced to America about 1843 by the Langenheim brothers of Philadelphia, enabled larger views to be made with sharper definition of detail in less time. Maguire was probably using the Voigtländer in 1844. Maguire and Jacobs were stocking them for sale by 1845. Improvements in the instruments and chemicals had reduced the exposure time from about half a minute to only a few seconds. Whereas in 1840 Lion could only take daguerreotype views because of the long exposure time required, by 1845 portraiture dominated the business in New Orleans and elsewhere in the country. *Le Courrier de la Louisiane* of July 9, 1845, noted the improvement also in the quality of the daguerreotypes produced. "When we compare the daguerreotypes of a few years past, with those which we obtain today, we can see what we may expect later. Families will appreciate the simple, rapid, sure and inexpensive way to reproduce features of those they love. The Daguerreotype has almost surpassed the Miniature."

New Orleans' economy was improving somewhat by 1845, and immigration continued at a steady pace. One observer noted: "The impression prevails very generally, in almost every section of this country, that wealth can be accumulated with great ease, and quite rapidly here, and this has caused a great excess of businessmen and much competition. Consequently profits are small, and but very few make annually more than enough to meet expenses, and many very soon become satisfied with the experiment of 'going south' to make a fortune."[28]

Several daguerreotypists were among the businessmen arriving in the city. Over a dozen new names appeared in the city directories and newspapers during the last half of the 1840s: C. E. Johnson, Charles Peyroux, G. Noessel, F. Boucher, A. D. Lansot, Felix Moissenet, R. Carr, P. Langlume, Samuel Moses, Mr. McLelland, E. White and Company, Ezekiel Hawkins, William W. Washburn, Mr. Franklin, L. P. David, the Plumbe Gallery, and H. Whittemore.

Whittemore and Hutchings advertised as partners in 1845 under the firm name Orleans Daguerrean Gallery, but the following year Whittemore was at another address, and by 1847 Hutchings was advertising his own "electro-magnetic portraits." Whittemore is perhaps the same H. W. Whittemore who exhibited forty views, including two of New Orleans, at the fair of the American Institute in 1851. Hutchings' "electroplating" was probably the method of adding more silver to the plates, instead of the coloring process mentioned on p. 36 herein.[29]

Shortly after Edward Jacobs began daguerreotyping in New Orleans, he formed a partnership with C. E. Johnson in the Southern Daguerreotype Portrait Gallery, which was at the corner of Camp and Canal streets, where many galleries were located through the years (10). Jacobs and Johnson claimed to have enlarged a window onto Canal Street that admitted the light necessary for portraits. On December 10, 1845, in the *Daily Picayune*, the Southern Daguerreotype Portrait Gallery invited "Citizens and strangers . . . to examine our NEW STYLE of *ne plus ultra* COLORED MINIATURES, surpassing any ever executed in this city, in *beauty*, *brilliancy* and *durability*. They are warranted imperishable, and taken without reversing the object." Perhaps this "new style" was related to Ezekiel Hawkins' visit to the city in December, 1845, when he also offered colored miniatures. Before Hawkins advertised in the New Orleans papers, Johnson

10. Canal Street, viewed from the corner of Camp Street, *ca.* 1847–1849. Copy of a daguerreotype; operator unknown.
Copy of original in Fotomuseum, Agfa-Gevaert A.G., Leverkusen-Bayerwerk, Germany, courtesy of International Museum of Photography at George Eastman House

and Jacobs had not mentioned colored miniatures in their advertisements. Hawkins' last announcement appeared December 7. At the 1846 fair Johnson and Jacobs received a Second Premium for their daguerreotypes, while Maguire again took the first prize.[30] Also in that year, the gallery claimed it was the sole agent in New Orleans for Langenheim's Patent Coloring Process, which had been patented that year.

The arrangement between Johnson and Jacobs was temporary, however, for Johnson advertised only as "Johnson and Co." in the spring of 1846. Apparently he quit the city in the summer, because in the fall E. White and Company was located on the same corner and called its gallery the Southern Daguerreotype Portrait Gallery.[31] E. White and Company offered daguerreotype supplies including plates by Scovill or from France, and of course their own "E. White" plates. Edward White, a maker of jewel cases in

1841, was a successful daguerrean and manufacturer of daguerreotype material in New York City during the 1840s. Usually local wholesalers had to go through New York in order to get their foreign or eastern-made products. To make a profit they had to charge higher prices than their suppliers. However, E. White and Company could offer to their New Orleans customers all equipment and materials, including their own plates, at a lower rate, thereby underpricing their competition.

In 1847 Jacobs was working for E. White and Company when he received praise for a daguerreotype portrait of General Zachary Taylor. The general's visit to New Orleans that December inspired the local artists to preserve his features. "He has been painted in oils, in water colors, at full length, half length, etc., down to the smallest locket miniature, through every variety of phase-profile, full face, etc., *ad infinitum*. Garbeille has modelled him in clay; De Chatillon has portrayed him on canvas. But it is our Daguerreotypists who have gone to work, *con amore*, to supply life-like representations of the Old Man Brave, to his multitudinous admirers."[32] Jacobs was deemed one of the daguerreotypists who had most successfully captured Taylor on his plate (11). The portrait is unusually powerful for its direct observation of the subject and penetration of character, and it is the outstanding extant portrait made in New Orleans to that date. Another distinguished portrait made by E. White and Company about the same time was of Captain Richard Caswell Gatlin, a native of North Carolina and graduate of West Point, who traveled through New Orleans after the Mexican War (12).[33]

The New Orleans newspapers were filled daily with news of the war in Mexico, and one even reported that G. Noessel, a local daguerrean, was in Vera Cruz "picking up interesting subjects with whose portraits to enrich his gallery." One such work was a daguerreotype of a Colonel Dominguez, "the commander of a spy company in General Scott's pay," whose predominant facial characteristic was, according to the *Daily Picayune* of Jan. 1, 1848, "coarse sensuality."

A few entrepreneurs established branches in several cities

11. Zachary Taylor, 1847. Whole-plate daguerreotype attributed to Edward Jacobs.
Chicago Historical Society

which were managed by trained operators. This system allowed the owner good prices on volume buying of supplies, but negligent management frequently forced branch operations into bankruptcy. At least one nationally known daguerrean opened a branch gallery in New Orleans during this period. John Plumbe established a "permanent branch of his justly celebrated Daguerrian Gallery" on Canal Street in the fall of 1844, but it lasted only one season. Plumbe at

12. Captain Richard Caswell Gatlin, 1847. Half-plate daguerreotype by E. White & Co.
North Carolina Division of Archives and History

that time offered instructions and the sale of apparatus.[34]

Ezekiel Hawkins, who became a well-known daguerreotypist in Cincinnati and a pioneer in albumen and collodion photography, opened a gallery at the corner of Canal Street and Exchange Place briefly in 1845. William W. Washburn, a native of New Hampshire, opened a gallery in New Orleans in the fall of 1849, calling it the New York Daguer-

13. A young girl, *ca.* 1845–1850. Sixth-plate daguerreotype attributed to Jules Lion.
Courtesy of Eugene R. Groves

rean Establishment; his brother Lorenzo joined him shortly thereafter as the director of the technical end of the business.[35]

In 1848 Jules Lion opened an art school on Exchange Alley in partnership with Dominique Canova. Though he no longer advertised daguerreotypes, Lion occasionally made them, including perhaps the portrait of the young girl of the Lion family, which dates from the late 1840s (13). The influence of photography was obvious in his lithographs from the period. On April 7, 1848, the *Bee* described his lithograph of General Taylor as having "absolutely the fidelity of a Daguerreotype."

In spite of the competition James Maguire managed to remain at the top of his profession in the city, and in 1845 he moved his gallery to 6 Camp Street (14). By 1847 he had evidently begun the association with William H. Harrington, who had not advertised in New Orleans since 1842, for in August, 1847, when he traveled to Nashville, Tennessee on a professional visit, he left Harrington in charge of his New Orleans gallery.[36] The Nashville *Daily Union* of September 29 praised Maguire as "the best artist in his line that has ever visited Nashville." Maguire returned to New Orleans in the fall. In 1847 he also made a portrait of Zachary Taylor. The *Daily Picayune* of January 11, 1848, called it "the best and most striking likeness of 'Old Zach' that we have yet seen of him anywhere." A contemporary daguerreotype copy of this portrait by the Boston photographers Southworth and Hawes is the only known visual reference to his daguerreotyping (15). Maguire's work was later used as the source of an engraving by T. B. Welch (16),

14. Advertisement for removal of Maguire's Daguerreotype Rooms, No. 6 Camp Street, *Daily Picayune*, October 16, 1845.
Louisiana Division, New Orleans Public Library

Removal.

MAGUIRE'S DAGUERREOTYPE ROOMS are removed to the south-east corner of Canal and Camp. Entrance No. 6 Camp street. Portraits guarantied perfect and satisfactory or no charge made.

APPARATUS with Instructions (guarantied the genuine Voigtlander Camera) for sale on reasonable terms; Plates, Cases, &c. &c., for sale at the lowest prices. o16 tf which appeared in James Herring's *National Portrait Gallery of Distinguished Americans* (1854).[37]

Again in 1849, Maguire received praise from the *Picayune* for his work in general, and one view in particular.

> Mr. Maguire, our resident daguerreotypist, has just executed a plate which we consider the *ne plus ultra* of excellence in the art of which he was, we believe, the founder in New Orleans. It is a representation of the inundated district of the city . . . taken from the cupola of the St. Charles Hotel. The scene is a beautiful, although a melancholy one. Common street flooded from almost the centre of the city to the swamp, seems a vast sheet of water, dotted here and there with skiffs that convey housekeepers to and from their inundated dwellings. . . . Mr. Maguire has really outdone himself in this effort, proving incontestably that in his specialty he need not fear a rival far or near.[38]

As this article reveals, Maguire was particularly bold with his advertising in the late 1840s, claiming incorrectly that he had introduced the daguerreotype into New Orleans. He also never failed to remind his patrons of the numerous awards he had received. But, he need not have feared an eclipse of fame, for in 1849 his esteem was further enhanced by yet another First Premium at the Agricultural and Mechanics' Association fair.[39]

By 1849, competition among suppliers was as fierce as that among the operators. Maguire was selling the Voigtländer camera "20% cheaper than any in the South. All other articles the same. Plates $2.50 per dozen, guaranteed the best plates made in the U.S. Cases at $2.75 and $3.50 per dozen. New York Cameras at $18." Maguire also claimed that he would promptly fill orders from rural areas.[40]

Within eight years, the daguerreotype was well established as the popular portrait medium in New Orleans. The directories listed over a dozen studios, which provided a service as well as an amusement to the Orleanians who strolled in to view the wares on display. In addition to those who catered to the city trade, some daguerreotypists equipped wagons for taking pictures in the country. On the

15. Zachary Taylor, *ca.* 1850. Sixth-plate daguerreotype; contemporary copy by Albert S. Southworth and Josiah J. Hawes, Boston, of the original daguerreotype by James Maguire.
Metropolitan Museum of Art, Gift of I. N. Phelps Stokes and the Hawes Family, 1937

16. Zachary Taylor, *ca.* 1854. Engraving by T. B. Welch, Philadelphia, from the daguerreotype by James Maguire.
National Portrait Gallery, Smithsonian Institution

rivers and bayous in the vicinity of New Orleans, some daguerreotypists put their equipment on flatboats, calling at wharves of plantations and small towns. Others set up their studios in boardinghouses or cheaply rented rooms.

By the end of the 1840s the daguerreotype era had reached its peak. However, this zenith was not to be long lasting. The introduction of new processes in the next decade would mark the decline of the use of the daguerreotype, though not its extinction.

III
New Processes and New Photographers

In 1850 New Orleans was the fifth largest city in the United States with a population over 116,000. The rate of growth was stabilizing because a majority of the immigrants were moving up the Mississippi River to fertile farming lands. The influx of Americans and foreigners, chiefly Irish and German, changed the ethnic caste of the city once again. And though the Creoles no longer dominated, numerically or economically, they did assert a cultural superiority with displays of fashions, attendance at operas and balls, and opulent celebrations at the Saint Charles and Saint Louis hotels, the social centers of the city. The gaiety and leisure of the city were offset with perennial epidemics; as the city's population swelled, yellow fever continued to be an alarming concern. In 1853, the year of the worst epidemic, over 10,000 people died.

Among those involved in city politics there was tension and bitterness, especially on the point of slavery. Portents of the Civil War had been evident in New Orleans since the late 1840s. Capitalizing on the decline of the Whigs in New Orleans, the highly chauvinistic Know-Nothing party moved in to gain control in the early fifties. By 1855 it was the most powerful group in the city, and by 1856 secessionist movements were quite strong in the state.

Economically, the city had made a recovery from the losses of the 1840s; bumper crops of cotton and cane bolstered the markets and contributed to the last phase of prosperity before the Civil War. The winter of 1859–1860 set a record for exports of cotton, tobacco, and sugar. New Orleans had little industry, only that required to fill local needs. Trade of goods from the Mississippi River Valley was the basis of the city's fortunes, but gradually the city lost some of that vital trade to the new midwestern railroads. In the early 1850s, several businessmen realized the future of the city lay in the development of its own rail systems; but capital was restricted after the 1837 crisis, and New Orleans could not develop them with the speed necessary to compete with Charleston, Savannah, or Saint Louis. James Robb planned three lines—two running to Texas and a third, the New Orleans, Jackson and Great Northern Railroad, which was to run to Chicago. By 1857 the Jackson Railroad, as it was called, was in bankruptcy; the next year, the line stretched only as far as Canton, Mississippi. With the loss of capital and the consequent loss of interstate trade, the city became increasingly provincial and self-protective in its relationships with the rest of the states.[1] Despite this setback, however, the city fathers were optimistic about the future, possibly because of the generally favorable climate and abundant crops of the 1850s.

The decade has been characterized as an era of "flush times, high wages, high profits, and high prices."[2] Such an atmosphere attracted all kinds of opportunists, including photographers, and stimulated the businesses already in operation. The overwhelming patronage accorded photographic portrait galleries was due, in part, to the proficiency and sometimes artistry of the well-trained operators. At first struggling to duplicate results achieved by Daguerre and other Europeans, Americans had worked industriously to improve equipment and techniques. Their achievements in the field were evident at the first world's exhibition held in 1851 at the Crystal Palace in London. The Americans took all the top honors in daguerreotyping and received critical praise as well. One writer for the *Illustrated London News* reported: "After a very minute and careful examination we are inclined to give America the first place. Whether the atmosphere is better adapted to the art, or whether the preparation of Daguerreotypes has been congenial with the tastes of the people, or whether they are unfettered with the patents in force in England, certain it is that the number of exhibitors has been very great and the quality of production super-excellent."[3]

Two years later, when America held its first world's fair—the Exhibition of the Industry of All Nations—in New York at its own Crystal Palace, the daguerreotype was still the most popular mode of portraiture. One New York newspaper estimated that about three million daguerreotypes were produced annually in America. Yet, in the next year the new albumen and collodion processes on glass and paper were introduced, quickly superseding the silverplate method, and gradually replacing it.

New Orleans photographers made the transitions to the new "types" soon after their appearance in other cities. Information was passed along by visiting operators and a few New Orleans photographers who frequently traveled to New York. New photography journals began circulating in the early 1850s: the *Daguerreian Journal*, later *Humphrey's Journal*, and the *Photographic Art-Journal*, later the *Photographic and Fine-Art Journal*.[4] Both magazines included articles contributed by the editors and by photographers from all over the country. The subjects of the articles varied, from advice on photographing children to detailed accounts of the steps involved in various photographic processes.

In early issues, each journal included a section that reported the whereabouts and activities of some of the country's daguerreotypists. The *Photographic Art-Journal*, in September, 1851, noted the presence in New York City of quite a number of western and southern daguerreans "who have come eastward for the purpose of purchasing their winter's supply of materials"; the list included Thomas Jefferson Dobyns of New Orleans. The 1850s also saw the introduction of American photography manuals. Henry Hunt Snelling, editor of the *Photographic Art-Journal*, published in 1849 *The History and Practice of the Art of Photography*, which was an immediate success. Journals and manuals functioned to provide helpful information for America's first photographers and a sense of community important to those persons who practiced the art throughout the nation.[5]

In New Orleans, as well as in the eastern cities, competition among daguerreotypists, assembly-line production, and reduced prices for equipment resulted in rampant price cutting for daguerreotypes. The better daguerreans resented the sale of inferior works by fraudulent methods and aligned themselves against the practice. A group of daguerreans from all over the country in 1851 formed the short-lived American Daguerre Association, initially the American Heliographic Association, whose objectives were: "to create in America, a higher standard of taste in the Heliographic art, to bring the Artists of our country in closer and more friendly intimacy, and to elevate and sustain the profession in the high rank it has attained." Dobyns, Albert Southworth of Boston, and Jeremiah Gurney of New York, were elected as vice-presidents of the association.[6] All over the country, no matter how remote the location, daguerreans who wished to maintain the appearance of high standards of workmanship articulated by the association, established themselves in elaborately outfitted salons and charged accordingly. The photography studio combined with an art gallery became a cultural institution.

Those photographers who were, according to the newspapers, most active in New Orleans in the decade before the war were William H. Harrington, Thomas J. Dobyns, Edward Jacobs, Felix Moissenet, William W. Washburn, John Hawley Clarke, F. S. Hedrick, Charles Marmu, Frederick Law, the Moses family—Samuel, Gustave, Bernard, Louis, and Edward—Samuel T. Anderson, and Samuel T. Blessing.

James Maguire's name is conspicuously absent from this list, as he died in January of 1851. The year before, he had formed a partnership with Harrington at 6 Camp Street where the two turned their attention to the practice of paper photography. The first paper process had been invented by W. H. Fox Talbot, who succeeded in making paper prints from paper negatives. His method, although patented in 1841 as the calotype, or talbotype, did not become popular in America because of the patent restrictions placed on it. Frederick and William Langenheim of Philadelphia secured the American patent from Talbot in May, 1849, a relatively long time after its introduction. The Langenheims encouraged the use of Talbot's process in the United States, but they were not successful in dissuading photographers from employing the daguerreotype process. In November of that year they sold what was probably the only franchise for the talbotype to Maguire and Harrington.[7]

This franchise provided for the exclusive use of the process in Louisiana, Alabama, Florida, Georgia, and Texas. Though they acquired the patent in November, 1849, Maguire and Harrington did not advertise the talbotype until March, 1850, when they listed all the advantages of the paper process over the daguerreotype. They noted that the image was "eminently susceptible of coloring . . . represents the sitter without any reverse effect . . . [and] can be duplicated to any extent without the additional trouble of another sitting." A *Daily Picayune* writer who had seen examples of the talbotype by Maguire and Harrington remarked, "It is a new department of photography, and the portraits recently taken by these gentlemen, according to this process, are peculiarly beautiful." The makers claimed that the talbotype could be "taken upon paper, ivory, glass, metal, and a variety of other substances," and announced they were prepared to give instructions and "ready to dispose of rights for the States specified." Maguire and Harrington also acquired from the Langenheims the right to make hyalotypes, positive pictures on glass, which had been made with glass negatives coated with albumen.[8] Thus Maguire and Harrington introduced both paper photography and photography on glass to New Orleans several years before either innovation would find popularity there.

At his death, Maguire was recognized as an excellent daguerreotypist, not only in New Orleans but also by the editor of the *Photographic Art-Journal*, who cited him as one of the operators who were responsible for the perfection of the daguerreotype art in America. Although he was very successful, Maguire left considerable debts.[9]

After Maguire's death, Harrington remained at 6 Camp Street; he was joined shortly by Thomas J. Dobyns, originally from Tennessee, who had galleries in Nashville and Louisville as well as New Orleans.[10] A daguerreotype por-

17. Two sisters, *ca.* 1850. Sixth-plate daguerreotype by Thomas J. Dobyns and William H. Harrington.
Collection of the International Museum of Photography at George Eastman House

trait of two unidentified ladies was made in their studio (17). In 1853 the firm, with a Mr. V. L. Richardson, opened a gallery in New York City and entered daguerreotypes in the world's fair there. Dobyns and Richardson, together with another Orleanian, Felix Moissenet, won an honorable mention for their specimens.[11]

Also in 1853 Harrington contributed a two-part article to *Humphrey's Journal* entitled "Hints on Practical Photography." The first part suggested a method for combating dampness, which prevented a clear impression on the plate. Noting that dampness "may occur in summer as well as in winter; the weather being warm or cold, wet or dry, clear or cloudy, raining or shining," Harrington provided a remedy that consisted of heating the plate above the temperature of the atmosphere of the room before polishing, and retaining that temperature during the process. He declared, "Since the adoption of this method, in connection with my partner, T. J. Dobyns, even in this humid climate of ours [New Orleans], when every thing in the room is dripping with moisture it has been attended with invariable success."[12]

In the second part of the article, Harrington gave instructions for taking stereoscopic pictures with the daguerreotype. After criticizing the usual stereoscopic daguerreotypes, particularly those brought from Europe, for the extravagant relief they exhibited when viewed through the stereoscope, Harrington presented a formula for correcting the excessive relief. He also presented his own design for a stereoscopic daguerreotype camera box, which enabled the operator to make two side-by-side pictures on the same plate, so that when viewed through the stereoscope, the two images merged optically to produce a three-dimensional effect.[13]

Stereoscopic daguerreotypes, and the stereoscope in general, were still a novelty to American photographers when Harrington published his article. Although it had become popular in Europe after its presentation at the Crystal Palace fair in London by the inventor Sir David Brewster, the stereoscope was not introduced in America until October, 1852; then only mild interest was shown. In the fall of 1853 Frederick Langenheim remarked that American photographers "have not paid the attention to the subject it richly deserves." At the time the Langenheim brothers were making glass stereographs by their patented hyalotype process. But even though daguerreotype stereographs were made (18), as well as those using the talbotype process and glass plates, none of these made the stereograph widely known in America. It was only the development of the wet-plate process that brought the stereograph, on paper particularly, into prominence and popularity.

Harrington could have been exposed to the stereoscopic method through the Langenheims or through his old friend Dr. Frederick Barnard, who also published an article in 1853 entitled "Method of Taking Daguerreotype Pictures for the Stereoscope, Simultaneously, upon the Same Plate, with an Ordinary Camera." Coincidentally, in his article on the stereoscope, Harrington in a note mentions his indebtedness "to Major J. G. Barnard, of the U.S. Army," for the rule of the parallel positions of the camera for the two views. Major John Gross Barnard happened to be Frederick's brother.[14]

In New Orleans, Harrington seems to have been one of the few interested in the stereoscope; not until December of 1854 does mention of it appear in local papers, and then in an advertisement by Gustave Moses. Moses, a New Orleans photographer, noted that the stereoscope was "somewhat novel here, but it is fully appreciated in the northern cities, as it imports capital likenesses." Whether Moses was advertising the daguerreotype stereograph, the glass stereograph, or even the card stereograph that the Langenheims had produced by that date, is not clear. Even though the Langenheims had been promoting their card stereographs in 1854, this new fashion did not really catch on in America until 1858. And advertisements for stereographs did not appear again in New Orleans until December of 1859.[15]

Dobyns, like Harrington, was active on a national level, acquiring galleries in several cities. In addition to his four other galleries, in February of 1854 he acquired one in Saint Louis and one that had belonged to the deceased Mr. Shaw in Memphis. However, within a year he disposed of all but his Memphis and New Orleans interests.[16]

During the 1850s Edward Jacobs acquired the position of dominance in New Orleans photography that Maguire had held during the 1840s. Jacobs began daguerreotyping in New Orleans about 1844 and was an operator for various firms through the decade. But by 1850 he had acquired enough capital to open his own gallery at 93 Camp Street in "Shiff's New Buildings" (19). The *Daily Picayune* paid a visit to the new rooms and reported the following: "Our old

18. A young lady, *ca.* 1853. Quarter-plate stereoscopic daguerreotype; operator unknown.
From the collections of the Louisiana State Museum

friend Mr. E. Jacobs, the celebrated daguerreotypist, so long and favorably known here, has removed his rooms to the fine new buildings in Camp street, just below Poydras; and has fitted up there with infinite taste a daguerrean gallery that cannot be surpassed for splendor and spacious accommodations by any establishment of the kind in the country. A saloon extending nearly the whole depth of the building, hung around with choice specimens of painting and daguerreotype, well lighted, adorned with great taste, is prepared for the reception of visitors, particularly the ladies."[17]

The daguerreotype room itself was lit from above and had a great variety of movable screens, ingeniously arranged to soften or increase the amount of light placed on the subject. The carpeted gallery was furnished with sofas from the celebrated New Orleans firm of P. Mallard and Company. In addition to his portrait service, Jacobs also supplied equipment at competetive prices.

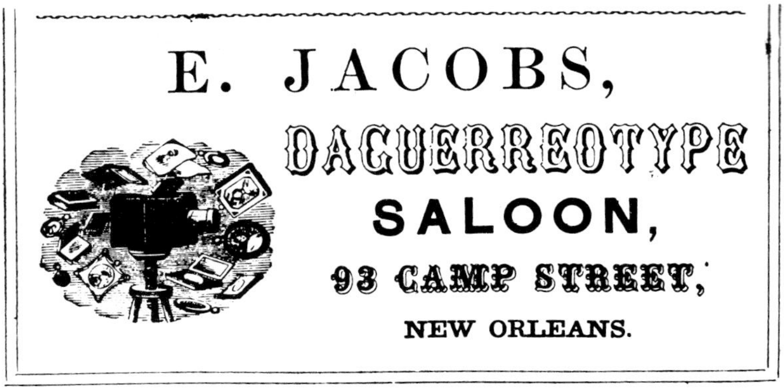

19. Advertisement in *Crescent City Business Directory*, 1858–59.
Louisiana Division, New Orleans Public Library

A writer for the *Courier* also inspected Jacobs' Daguerreotype Saloon, afterward calling it "one of the most superb establishments of the kind we ever saw; indeed we may, with perfect propriety, say that it is the finest in the United States, and we doubt whether it is surpassed by any in the world." The paper was also pleased that Jacobs had "the good taste" not to exhibit his own specimens, because "his reputation is already so well established that he can dispense with such exhibitions." That Jacobs' reputation was well established was also apparent by the fact that *Humphrey's Journal* noted his appearance in New York and called him one of "our first Daguerreotypists." In another issue of the *Journal*, one writer commented that he had seen one of Jacobs' daguerreotype specimens and that it "does credit alike to the operator and the art."[18] The praise was well deserved, for Jacobs' daguerreotype portraits were among the finest made in New Orleans (20).

In New Orleans Jacobs' popularity seemed to be due not only to his work but also to the fact that he was a permanent artist in that city. The author of an article reprinted in *Humphrey's Journal* made the point that "Mr. Jacobs is not a Northern star, merely paying us a visit for the sake of a few dollars, to be picked up during the winter, put into a bag, and carried to the fashionable summer resorts. We regard him, or rather his establishment, as an institution, and one

20. A gentleman, *ca.* 1850. Quarter-plate daguerreotype by Edward Jacobs.
Courtesy of Billy Wolf

of the noblest in New Orleans. Daguerreotype galleries we have plenty of, but we have only one Jacobs."[19]

Respect for Jacobs and his work by the local community probably contributed to the selection of daguerreotypes by Jacobs to be used as the basis for engravings that appeared in *Cohen's New Orleans Directory* for 1854 and 1855. These were engravings of leading citizens and were accompanied by biographical sketches. Jacobs was acknowledged as the original artist (21), as Harrington had been earlier in

Cohen's New Orleans and Lafayette Directory for 1852, for the plate of J. T. Hammond.

Jacobs' gallery was a popular place with the citizens because he not only had a daguerreotype department, but he also had a Gallery of Fine Arts that exhibited colored engravings, statuary, including "busts and full lengths of Shakespeare," and other works of art. There was no admission charge to view these works. This display of fine art filled a void in the cultural life of the city, for New Orleans had few art galleries.

21. D. O. Hincks. Engraving after a daguerreotype by Edward Jacobs in *Cohen's New Orleans Directory*, 1855.
From the collections of the Louisiana State Museum

Jacobs, like Dobyns and Harrington and other owners of large daguerreotype establishments, employed assistants, but he maintained that he supervised all the work done at his gallery. Though most customers were satisfied with the work done there, not all were. In one incident, two ladies came to the studio to have a picture of an infant taken. "It is difficult to take a good picture and the ladies were hard to please; Mr. Jacobs got vexed and excited; they said he didn't know how to treat ladies; he replied he knew very well how to treat *ladies* when they came to his rooms." The ladies were insulted and returned home to report their "mistreatment" to one of their husbands, who, with a friend, went to Jacobs' establishment. An argument ensued and the husband attempted to stab Jacobs; he was charged with assault with intent to murder.[20]

Felix Moissenet, originally from France, was another early daguerrean who operated a popular studio in the 1850s. In 1849 he had a daguerreotype saloon at the corner of Royal and Saint Louis streets in the Vieux Carré, but in 1850 he opened a new studio at 28 Camp Street in the American Sector. He had just returned from a visit to Europe where he had "made himself thoroughly acquainted with the latest improvements in the Daguerrean art, and selected the best instruments."[21] Like Lion and Maguire before them, several New Orleans operators such as Moissenet and Jacobs felt it necessary to go to Europe for the latest improvements. The experience, no doubt, heightened Moissenet's reputation among his patrons (22). In 1851 Moissenet moved his studio again, this time to the corner of Camp and Canal streets, where he made the group portrait of the six young gentlemen (23). Moissenet also enjoyed a reputation for his work outside New Orleans. In 1850 he was listed in the *Daguerreian Journal* directory, and in 1853 he shared with Dobyns and Richardson the honorable mention award at the world's fair.

Another daguerrean who came from Europe was Samuel W. Moses, who was a chemist in his native Germany before immigrating to Louisiana in the 1830s. Family tradition reports that he intended to work in the Louisiana sugar

22. A young lady, *ca.* 1850. Quarter-plate daguerreotype by Felix Moissenet.
Historic New Orleans Collection

industry, but in late 1849 he opened a daguerreotype studio at 230 Royal Street. Then in 1850 he was located at the corner of Camp and Poydras streets, where he remained for the next ten years. Samuel trained his four sons—Louis, Bernard, Edward R., and Gustave—all of whom became successful operators. Before the end of the 1850s, there were three Moses establishments along Camp Street, from Poydras to Canal Street.[22]

There were a dozen popular galleries along Camp Street in the fifties. One of the most notable was that of William

W. Washburn, the New York Daguerrean Establishment, at 29 Camp Street. Washburn was drawing on his experience as an operator in New York when he styled his gallery.[23] The *Daily Picayune* of November22, 1849, noted that he had "enjoyed a high reputation in New York for skill and proficiency in his profession." He made a specialty of photographing visiting celebrities. One of the first and most famous of all was Jenny Lind, the Swedish soprano, who came to the city in 1850. Shortly after her arrival, Miss Lind sent her secretary to all the daguerreotype galleries in the city for samples of their work; she chose Washburn's gallery to take her portrait. No doubt this *coup* enhanced Washburn's career. In 1851, he moved his studio to 26 Camp Street, and two years later he established himself in the fashionable new Touro Buildings on Canal Street, where he continued to make superb portraits (24) and operate a

23. Pierre Adolph Hebrard, Jr., Paul Boudousquie, Richard Hebrard, Numa Perilliat, Ernest Miltenberger, and Ernest Ducatel, *ca.* 1850. Whole-plate daguerreotype by Felix Moissenet.
From the collections of the Louisiana State Museum

24. Lady with a bonnet, *ca.* 1850. Sixth-plate daguerreotype by William W. Washburn.
Courtesy of Richard T. Rosenthal

photographic supply business. He proudly advertised his new Daguerrean Saloon as the "most eligible location in the city, and for elegance in the fitting up, surpasses anything in the Southern country." Washburn had just returned from a recent trip to the northern cities and claimed to have learned of all the new improvements in his field.[24]

Until 1854 New Orleans photographers, with the exception of Maguire and Harrington, had promoted only the daguerreotype. Then in December of that year two advertisements appeared for photographs on paper. On December 24 the *Daily Picayune* devoted a full column on the front page to the history of the photographic art in general, and to Jacobs in particular. After describing the beginnings of the art with the daguerreotype, the article then discussed the talbotype.

> One of the most valuable improvements in this beautiful art is that for which the world is indebted to Mr. Talbot, the inventor of the process called the *Talbotype*; by means of which the photograph, being taken from the living head, may be produced therefrom, on paper, to the extent of hundreds of impressions; and these, colored from life, may be made to resemble the finest miniatures on ivory. . . . Within a year or two great improvements in Talbotyping have been made. Though we have seen many specimens of it we have met with none in any part of the country to equal those which Mr. Jacobs, the well-known photographer in this city, is now, after long and costly preparation, producing at his rooms in Camp street. He has brought this style of taking photographs . . . [to the] height of perfection.

Jacobs, it seems, was contributing to what Welling calls "a mild flourishing of the calotype practice," taking place in America during these early years of the decade. In July, *Humphrey's Journal* began a series of articles on the talbotype that presented "the improvement up to the present date."[25] It is not clear from the *Picayune* article what method of improvement on the talbotype Jacobs was implementing; he may have been using the calotype process introduced in 1851 by the Frenchman Gustave LeGray, who modified Talbot's process with the use of a thinner paper saturated with wax.

An advertisement in *Le Courrier*, which appeared four days before Jacobs', asserted that "for more than two years, portraits are taken in Paris on paper only." One of the two gentlemen who placed this advertisement, M. Marma [Charles Marmu], was said to have been a successful operator in Paris whom Mr. Picard, his partner who lived in New Orleans, had persuaded to come to the Crescent City. Proclaiming that "the plate has done its time," Picard and

Marmu spoke of all the advantages of paper photography, as had Maguire and Harrington four years earlier: several prints could be made from one negative; the portrait could be retouched if it proved initially unacceptable; and there was no reverse effect. What was different from Maguire and Harrington and Jacobs was that Picard and Marmu were using, not the talbotype or calotype, but a collodion process.

The Englishman Frederick Scott Archer had developed a process for making photographs on glass coated with collodion. When Archer's process for making paper prints from collodion negatives became known in France, it was readily adopted, because photographers there had become used to the paper process with the calotype method. The collodion method was preferred because it had the advantage of being much faster, from exposure through development.

Although Picard and Marmu's advertised claims were supported by an editorial report in the December 21 *Courrier*, which admitted the superiority of paper photographs over the daguerreotype, the firm apparently existed only one season. Marmu eventually opened his own gallery in 1857, and it became a familiar sight in the French Quarter.

Because Archer had not restricted the use of his process, which he published in 1851, his work became the basis for several experiments in America. From the experiments of Dr. Giles Langdell of Boston and Dr. Charles M. Cresson of Philadelphia, James A. Cutting, a Boston photographer, became aware of a formula that combined bromide of potassium with collodion to make a glass negative from which paper positives could be made. Seizing a business opportunity, Cutting appropriated the idea, patented it in July of 1854, and took the credit for making collodion portraiture commercially practical.[26]

Several other photographers in America, especially in Boston and Philadelphia, had also been conducting their own experiments with paper prints. In 1850 John Whipple of Boston patented a process to make positive paper prints that he called crystalotypes, which were made from a glass negative coated with albumen. But by the summer of 1853

Whipple had substituted collodion and was offering instructions to other photographers.

The early paper prints made from the collodion negatives were made on smooth paper prepared with the use of common salt and referred to as "plain salted paper." These plain-salt prints were various shades of brown, as they were toned with gold chloride after their preparation. The plain paper was an excellent surface for receiving paint, and thus photographers often painted over these photographs with pigment or India ink.

Paper photography was quickly gaining advocates. According to the *Photographic Art-Journal* of April, 1854, "There have been more apparatus sold in the United States the last three months for paper manipulation than during the whole time previous since its discovery." However, the daguerreotype still remained the popular medium for portrait photography. When *Humphrey's Journal* was asked in the early fall of 1854 whether pictures upon glass and paper would ever entirely supersede the daguerreotype, the answer was an unequivocal no.[27]

Still, photographers were interested in exploring other means of taking portraits. Jacobs, who in the winter of 1854 was making calotypes, also offered a new type of photograph during that season. This was a photograph on ivory instead of paper, which the *Picayune* called "The Most Perfect Photograph Yet." Jacobs' ivory process predated the English ivorytype, patented in October of 1855 by John Mayall, and the American ivorytype, introduced during the autumn of 1855. His may have been similar to the pictures on ivory produced by the Langenheim brothers by 1852.[28]

In October of 1855, Jacobs announced that he was practicing "all the new Processes" and was prepared to take photographs, either plain or colored, and ambrotypes, which he described as "a new and beautiful style of portraits impressed on glass prepared in a peculiar manner" (25).[29] At the time that Cutting secured his patent for paper prints, he obtained another patent for a thin collodion negative on glass, which was given the name ambrotype by the daguer-

25. Young man with a badge, *ca.* 1855. Half-plate ambrotype by Edward Jacobs.
Courtesy of Eugene R. Groves

rean Marcus A. Root. When the negative image was backed by a black material and viewed by reflected light, a positive picture was obtained. Like the daguerreotype, the ambrotype was a one-of-a-kind image; that is, it could not be duplicated, as could paper images printed from a glass negative. Ambrotypes were made in the same standard sizes as daguerreotypes and mounted and framed in the same manner.

By the winter of 1855, ambrotypes were becoming known to the public and preferred by some to the daguerreotypes because they did not have to be held at a particular

26. John Ryan Carroll, *ca.* 1855. Half-plate ambrotype; photographer unknown.
From the collections of the Louisiana State Museum

angle to be viewed, and they were cheaper. However, the image quality, the rendition of detail and clarity of tones, was inferior to that of the daguerreotype. Nevertheless, practically all the operators in New Orleans offered the ambrotype in the winter of 1856. Like the daguerreotype, the ambrotype was used primarily for portraiture, whether it be of the living (26 and 27) or of the dead (28).

Among the old operators there was no doubt a prejudice against the new and cumbersome method of collodion, or

27. A servant of the Carroll family, *ca.* 1855. Quarter-plate ambrotype; photographer unknown.
From the collections of the Louisiana State Museum

wet-plate photography, so named because the plate had to be kept damp through the entire exposure and development process. It was messy and it required an investment in more equipment. Despite the competition from the ambrotype and the paper photograph, daguerreotypes remained a feature of the established New Orleans galleries. Neither could surpass the daguerreotype for its sharp mirrorlike image (29 and 30).

Paper photography began its true ascendancy in New Orleans in 1856, the year that John Hawley Clarke, a native of Delaware, and Samuel T. Anderson and Samuel T. Blessing, both of Texas, began practicing there. Clarke received his tutelage as an operator from Marcus Root in Washington, D.C., and could have learned the collodion process from Cutting at Root's gallery in 1853. A letter from S. Rush Seibert to Dr. Samuel Busey confirms his whereabouts at that time. "During the winter of 1851 and 1852 I negotiated with him [Mr. N. S. Bennett] for the purchase of the gallery for Marcus A. Root and John H. Clark, who immediately obtained possession and refitted the skylight and rooms, and there produced many fine specimens of the Daguerrean art." Root himself verified that this was indeed the John Clarke who later worked in New Orleans. "In 1852 I opened a gallery in Washington, D.C., under the care of a

28. Mourning portrait of a deceased child, *ca.* 1855. Half-plate ambrotype; photographer unknown.
Anonymous collection

former pupil of mine, John Clark, who, at this date (1863), has a flourishing establishment in New Orleans."[30]

Clarke undoubtedly gained much valuable experience from the great Philadelphia daguerreotypist, and if Seibert's statements are accurate, Clarke had the opportunity to become familiar with Cutting's process at a very early stage. According to Seibert, Cutting came to Washington in 1853 to apply for a patent "for the use of collodion for a coating upon glass on which pictures can be made." Seibert stated that Cutting used a darkroom in the Root and Clarke establishment "and there prepared the plates for the first negative made upon collodion film in this city."[31]

In New Orleans Clarke became associated with F. S. Hedrick, who advertised himself as "daguerrean and ambrotypist" and whose establishment at 26 Camp Street, at the corner of Common, was said to have "the best and largest skylights in the city" (31). After Clarke's arrival, the firm advertised "photographs from life or copied from old da-

29. Henry Carroll at ages six and thirteen, *ca*. 1853–1860. Quarter-plate daguerreotypes; operator unknown.
From the collections of the Louisiana State Museum

guerreotypes, plain, touched in india ink or colored in oil or watercolor."[32] India ink, as applied to the portrait of Mr. Paulsen, added a velvety tone to the finished print (32). Watercolor was added for the patrons who wished their portraits to have more the appearance of a traditional painting (33); however, the results did not always meet expectations.

The partnership with Hedrick did not last long, for Hedrick was operating alone in the latter part of 1857. Clarke then opened his own establishment on Canal Street. He had

30. An invalid boy of the Harris family, *ca.* 1855–1860. Sixth-plate daguerreotype; operator unknown.
From the collections of the Louisiana State Museum

31. A young woman, *ca.* 1855–1859. Ninth-plate daguerreotype by F. S. Hedrick.
From the collections of the Louisiana State Museum

apparently proven his superior ability in a short time, for he was able to attract talented associates, especially a fine watercolorist (34). In August of 1858, R. A. Carnden commended Clarke in the *Photographic and Fine-Art Journal.* "J. H. CLARK'S [*sic*] Gallery at No. 94 Canal Street, deserves especial notice from the good display of plain photographs, and those in water colors. The latter are deservedly fine, as Mr. Clark possesses the best water color artist in New Orleans. His photographic artist was in E. Jacob's [*sic*] employ for some months, and Clark bids fair to rival all other galleries, as his reputation is constantly on the increase, and his facilities keep pace with his reputation. Only photographs and ambrotypes are taken at this gallery." Carnden also

32. Louis Paulsen, *ca.* 1857. Salted-paper photograph by John H. Clarke.
From the collections of the Louisiana State Museum

noted that the journal for which he was writing was to be found in New Orleans only in Clarke's establishment, and thus his pictures were "more in accordance with the improvements now known in the art."[33]

Anderson and Blessing were already established in Galveston, Texas, when in 1856 they opened a New Orleans gallery at 120 Canal that they had purchased from Washburn.[34] Anderson and Blessing dealt in every style of photography but specialized in collodion photography at an early date. They advertised in *Mygatt's New Orleans Directory* for 1857 that "having devoted fifteen months' specially to Ambrotyping, [we] are prepared to take them Superior to any other Pictures." They also excelled in paper photography finished in oil, pastel, or watercolor. A specialty of the firm in 1857, at their new gallery at 134 Camp Street (35) was the life-size or colossal print.

Early attempts to make large photographs followed French methods, which employed huge cameras; however, an easier method of obtaining mammoth photographs was with an enlarging camera. The most widely used was the solar camera patented by David A. Woodward of Baltimore early in 1857. These immense photographs were made not only on paper but on canvas, after which they were usually colored to resemble oil paintings. One commentator later

33. The Gasquet family, *ca.* 1857. Painted salted-paper photograph by John H. Clarke.
From the collections of the Louisiana State Museum

34. Woman with a bonnet, *ca.* 1857. Painted salted-paper photograph by John H. Clarke.
From the collections of the Louisiana State Museum

wrote: "Photography has gone still further, and life-size pictures are now produced which, when painted by the skilful [*sic*] artist, have rivalled the creations of most painters. . . . The last great achievement of the Photographic Art, is the production of life-size, full-length portraits . . . accomplished by the means of the new solar camera, 'lately introduced.'"[35] Many life-size photographs lie undetected behind paint; many photographers succeeded in disguising their art well.

According to Carnden, Anderson and Blessing produced "the largest photographs from life in New Orleans." And in both their Galveston and New Orleans branches, the firm offered a large assortment of photographic supplies. Carnden noted this and added, "Their trade in this line is considerable." In the earlier years of photography, operators purchased supplies on yearly trips to New York, where they acquired equipment for themselves and usually a surplus for other local photographers; they also ordered supplies by telegraph. With the introduction of the collodion processes and the growing popularity of the medium came the development of new products and a larger market for all types of photographic equipment. The leading eastern supply houses, E. and H. T. Anthony and Company and Scovill Company, sent representatives to the southern and western states to create new markets for their products. The firm of Anderson and Blessing, and later Blessing's own firm, remained an important photographic supplies depot throughout the 1850s and 1860s.

With so many galleries in New Orleans there were bound to be disagreements among colleagues. In early 1857 Theodore M. Schleier had an ambrotype and photographic gallery on Chartres Street. James Andrews had his gallery at the corner of Canal and Saint Charles. Evidently the two had an argument that resulted in Andrews' attacking Schleier at his establishment with a poker. The February 13 issue of the *Courier* commented drolly that such an action prevented Mr. Schleier from carrying on his business; however, both remained in the profession in New Orleans for the next few years.

Also in 1857 William H. Abrams advertised the melainotype, or tintype, another collodion process that used a thin iron plate instead of glass to support the emulsion.[36] The plate was japanned black before exposure to provide a ground for the negative image. The tintype was more durable and cheaper than glass and like the ambrotype was a unique image. However, it was frequently made with a multilens camera that produced several images upon a single plate, thereby making it more of a bargain than the ambrotype. Abrams, who remained in the city until the Civil War, was an early promoter of the tintype, though it did not really become popular until the 1860s.

Dobyns and Harrington, who in 1856 were still advertising daguerreotype portraits, joined the number of photographers interested in photography on glass. They said that they preferred this latter method to paper photography, because "the chief objection to Photography, colored either in watercolors or oil, even by the most able artist, is the liability to alter the expression of the likeness." Harrington may have been prejudiced against paper photography after the poor reception of the talbotype, which he and Maguire had offered earlier. In addition to the ambrotype, they offered heliographs, or colored pictures on glass. The inventor Ezekiel Hawkins was a guest operator in their studio during the spring of 1856. It was claimed that through his heliographic process, the image was indelibly fixed upon glass,

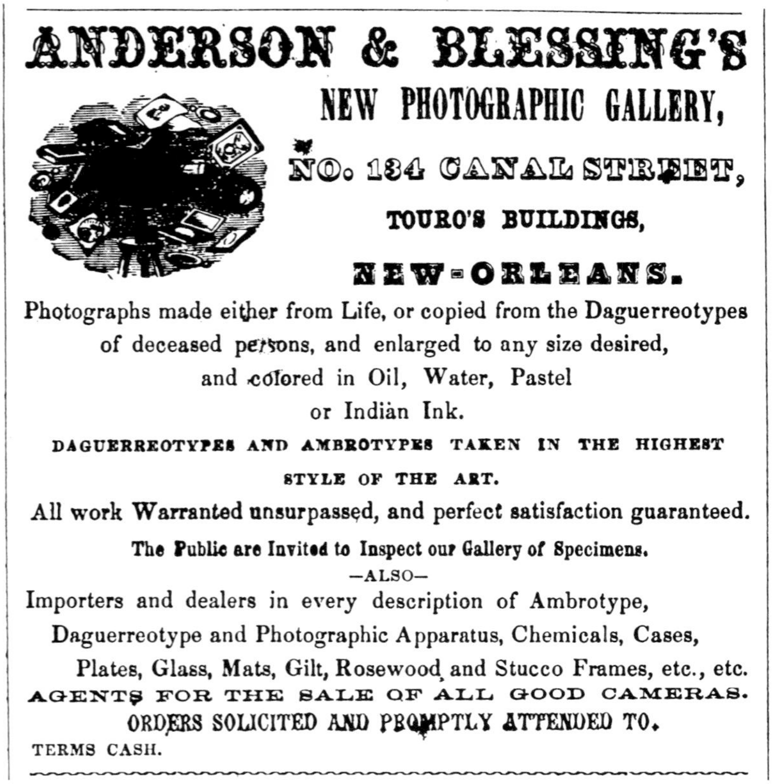
ANDERSON & BLESSING'S
NEW PHOTOGRAPHIC GALLERY,
NO. 134 CANAL STREET,
TOURO'S BUILDINGS,
NEW-ORLEANS.
Photographs made either from Life, or copied from the Daguerreotypes of deceased persons, and enlarged to any size desired, and colored in Oil, Water, Pastel or Indian Ink.
DAGUERREOTYPES AND AMBROTYPES TAKEN IN THE HIGHEST STYLE OF THE ART.
All work Warranted unsurpassed, and perfect satisfaction guaranteed.
The Public are Invited to Inspect our Gallery of Specimens.
—ALSO—
Importers and dealers in every description of Ambrotype, Daguerreotype and Photographic Apparatus, Chemicals, Cases, Plates, Glass, Mats, Gilt, Rosewood and Stucco Frames, etc., etc.
AGENTS FOR THE SALE OF ALL GOOD CAMERAS.
ORDERS SOLICITED AND PROMPTLY ATTENDED TO.
TERMS CASH.

35. Advertisement, in *Crescent City Business Directory*, 1858–59.
Louisiana Division, New Orleans Public Library

with the natural colors, "while no paint is applied to the picture." Hawkins had operated a daguerreotype gallery in New Orleans at the beginning of his career. He later moved to Cincinnati, where he experimented with collodion as early as 1847. His heliograph may have been a photograph on glass sensitized with albumen or collodion, or it may have been similar to the diaphanotype, which he patented in 1857. This was a paper print that was attached to a plate glass with balsam and then tinted with oil colors.[37]

Before Anderson and Blessing and before Woodward's patented solar camera, Dobyns and Harrington had offered life-size photographs on canvas to their patrons. But with all these novelties the fortunes of the firm were soon in decline. A fire in the chemical room of their gallery destroyed much of their equipment and caused three thousand dollars' worth of damages in January of 1857.[38] Despite the losses the two remained in business for another two years, supplementing their works with photographs from New York galleries, a practice for which Carnden criticized them. "From the extensive display at the door one would infer that the work up-stairs would excel all others in New Orleans; but on viewing the specimens on exhibition, I was more surprised to discover that they were the productions of Mr. BRADY, of New York, from the fact of the mats being stamped with his name—indicating that New York Ambrotypes were preferred in New Orleans instead of their own work."[39]

According to Carnden the establishment was being run by T. A. Gray, which may have contributed to the seeming lack of quality in the gallery. Gray, in Carnden's words, lacked the requisite photographic skill to operate successfully the firm's solar camera, which he allowed to lie "amongst the rubbish of the gallery." The firm of Dobyns and Harrington came to an end when Dobyns retired in 1859. *Gardner's New Orleans Directory* for 1860 listed him only at his residence in Amite City, Louisiana; he had been purchasing land in Saint Helena Parish since 1855 and then in 1859 bought a house in Amite. Harrington worked alone as an ambrotypist for another year in the city but then ceased to advertise after 1860. He had worked in New

36. Daguerreian Gallery, corner of Camp and Canal streets, *ca.* 1858. Copy (*ca.* 1900) of ambrotype attributed to Frederick Law.
From the collections of the Louisiana State Museum

Orleans in the photographic arts for almost twenty years.[40]

Moissenet was another photographer whose career in New Orleans terminated at the end of the decade. For two years, 1856 and 1858, he was in partnership with Frederick Law at the corner of Camp and Canal streets. Then Law took over the gallery, which by Carnden's account became long known as a "Daguerreian Gallery" (36). In 1858 Moissenet joined William W. Washburn at his establishment on Canal Street but he was not listed in the city directories after 1861.[41] Law, however, remained at his famous corner, making admirable daguerreotypes (37) and photographs.

Jacobs' gallery remained one of the best known in the city. While continuing a daguerreotype service, his gallery achieved an excellent reputation for ambrotypes and paper prints. In October, 1856, he was commissioned by the Continental Guard of the city to create a memorial portrait, a painted photograph, of Charles Callahan.[42] A newspaper

37. Portrait of young boy, by the Anthony process of vignetting, *ca.* 1858–1860. Sixth-plate daguerreotype by Frederick Law.
Courtesy of Billy Wolf

correspondent, Callahan had been killed while on assignment in Havana during the expedition of Narcisco Lopez to Cuba. Jacobs still had his gallery of fine arts, which Carnden emphasized in his description of Jacobs' establishment. "In reality, it is more a gallery devoted to the exhibition of splendid Oil Paintings by the old masters, than a Photographic Gallery. He has imported a large collection of rare works from Europe at a considerable expense, and takes much pride in the display. His attention is consequently directed from the art photographic."[43] Though Carnden's criticism was probably overstated, Jacobs was intensely interested in the fine arts and in 1858 sold his gallery to L. S. Lipman and left the city to study painting in Europe. Upon his return in September, 1859, he advertised that he would paint miniatures on ivory in oils and that he was a professor of art. However, he also took a position at Lipman's gallery, having returned "with all the latest improvements in the photographic art." Jacobs' popularity is indicated by the *Picayune*'s comment, "Of course, there'll be a rush there by his scores of friends to see the 'returned one,' and welcome him back."[44]

By the end of the 1850s New Orleans' population had grown to approximately 150,000. There were six or seven fashionable saloons that the citizenry patronized for their displays of art as well as to have portraits taken. Clarke's, Anderson and Blessing's, Dobyns and Harrington's, Moissenet's, Washburn's, and Jacobs' were all popular places for socializing and amusement. There were perhaps twenty additional galleries. Besides Andrews and Schleier, other operators were Messrs. Jackson, Ranney, and Gustafson; Giroux and Hirsch; P. Camille; J. H. Frobus; John E. Hulbert; and William Guay, who in 1856 with W. E. Mealy had the Economic Daguerreotype Gallery, which advertised daguerreotypes complete in cases for only fifty cents.[45]

Even though New Orleans operators like Guay and Mealy still clung to the daguerreotype during the 1850s, new chemical and mechanical technology had led to the introduction of albumen and collodion photography and the paper print, which would come into its own during the next decade and eventually replace all other styles of the photographic arts.

IV
Diversity and Prosperity Before the War

New Orleans by 1860 had grown to a city of 170,000, almost half of whom were foreign born, with those of Irish, German, and French origin dominating the immigrant population. During the winter season, another 35,000 transients arrived looking for occupations on the river, in a trade, or in the arts. In the early part of 1860, commerce in the port was at its peak; the volume of trade equaled that of New York City. But New Orleans was troubled; the unstable political climate of the previous decade had intensified. Local newspapers added fuel to the fire with pro-Secessionist sentiments. By the winter of 1860–1861, the economy began to turn. Banks took a cautious stance and stopped all loans; imports declined and prices rose.

At the beginning of the decade, about forty photographers were listed in the city directories. Among them were the familiar names of Jacobs, Washburn, the Moses family, John Clarke, and Anderson and Blessing. Certainly others arrived as part of the transient population. In *Gardner's New Orleans Directory* for 1860, most operators listed themselves as daguerreans or ambrotypists, though collodion photography was making a serious challenge as the favored method of most operators.

By 1860 photographers all over the country had become incensed by the continuing controversy over the patent rights of James A. Cutting. Suits had been filed against operators whom Cutting accused of infringement, but these had been settled out of court. The national photographic community maintained that the specific techniques which Cutting had patented in 1854 had been widely used and published before that date and that the patents given Cutting were therefore fraudulent. At a meeting in New York on February 3, 1860, an organization of photographers and suppliers declared their solidarity against Cutting and formed a committee to solicit funds for the defense of the latest case, proclaiming that all photographers in America were obligated to lend assistance, because the "destiny of the photographic art is at stake." Anderson and Blessing and Harrington were designated agents to collect subscriptions in New Orleans.[1] The use of collodion was so widespread that to enforce the payment of royalties to Cutting would have crippled the industry. The Cutting problem remained an issue until 1868, when the reversal of the patent settled it.

Collodion or wet-plate processes were preferred especially by those making outdoor views. With large plate-glass negatives and a new type of lens, photographers were able to record scenes in sharp detail, free of distorted perspective. In 1860, Charles C. Harrison and J. Schnitzer of New York developed the Globe lens, which quickly became the international standard for landscapes, as the Petzval lens had for portraits.[2] Large glossy paper prints were made on albumen-coated paper, which Americans began using about 1860; these were durable and inexpensive to make.

Two photographers who specialized in outdoor photography at an early date were Jay D. Edwards, a native of New Hampshire who arrived in New Orleans in 1859, and Edward Jacobs. In the summers of 1859 and 1860 Edwards made views of the United States Custom House, which was under construction on Canal Street. These were ordered by the Department of the Treasury, one of four government offices employing photographers at that date.[3] Thomas K. Wharton, the architect in charge, sent twenty-three of Edwards' views to Howell Cobb, secretary of the Treasury. At the same time, Edwards also made twelve views of the United States Marine Hospital, located below the city at Chalmette, which was being repaired by the Department of the Army. In the summer of 1860, Major P. G. T. Beauregard, then the superintendent of the Army Engineers for the

38. New Custom House, New Orleans, under construction, June 30, 1860. Albumen photograph by J. D. Edwards.
Department of Archives and Manuscripts, Troy H. Middleton Library, Louisiana State University

southern states, sent another group of Edwards' photographs with his annual report to Cobb (38 and 39).[4] In Europe photography had been used to document public buildings for government agencies and to record the construction of such buildings as the Crystal Palace in London. Ten years later the United States government began making instantaneous pictorial records of their important projects.

Edwards may have operated from a wagon or tent in 1859 and 1860, for he was not in the directories. Also, his early trade labels, which advertised rural as well as urban views, imported views, and stereograph cards, indicate that he was a more mobile and adverturesome photographer than most of his colleagues. "FROM J. D. EDWARD'S GALLERY OF PHOTOGRAPHIC ART. Views of New Orleans, the Bayous, Swamps and Shell Piles of Louisiana, Lowel [*sic*] Cotton Factories, Niagria [*sic*] Falls, Mount Vernon, Washington, Philadelphia, New York, Boston, Providence, R.I., Harvard College, Cambridge, Mass., New Hampshire,

39. New Custom House, June, 1860. Albumen photograph by J. D. Edwards.
Department of Archives and Manuscripts, Troy H. Middleton Library, Louisiana State University

Montreal and Quebec, Canada, St. Louis, Mo., Constantinople, Turkey, Rome, etc., etc. for sale at the Gallery cheap. Stereoscopic views of any part of the world obtained to order." Edwards also advertised "Views of Stores, Dwellings, Steamboats, etc., taken to order on short notice." In the portrait department, he offered "Old Likenesses enlarged to life size and painted in oil, water or pastel. Likeness and durability guaranteed. Ambrotypes, Photographs, Melainotypes, and all other kinds of pictures taken in the first style of the art, and warranted at less prices than any other gallery in the south. Full instructions given in the art to Ladies and Gentlemen, Apparatus furnished, terms very moderate. Post Office Address J. D. Edwards, Box E. No. 12, New Orleans, La."[5]

By the spring of 1861, Edwards had established a gallery at 19 Royal Street, where he continued his specialty in outdoor views. On April 9, the *Daily Picayune* reported that he had shown them "six beautiful photographic views of the Park of New Orleans [City Park], the Metairie Ridge and the Metairie race course, the latter taken on Saturday, when Lightning surprised so many sportsmen by beating Planet." These too were for sale at his gallery.

In 1860, Jacobs also made views of the Custom House (40). Whereas the surviving views by Edwards are of a documentary nature, recording details of construction from the exterior, Jacobs' surviving view of the interior of the great hall is romantic, reminiscent of the work of his European contemporaries. He dramatized the monumental proportions of the Greek Revival interior elements, displaying a certain artistic flair with architectural photography, much as he did with portraiture.

Jacobs was still at 93 Camp Street in October, 1860, when he offered a new style of photography, the ivorytype. The *Daily Picayune*, ever eager to pay a compliment to Jacobs, commented that at his art gallery, "where we are always being invited to mark some new and valuable improvement in the art and science of sun-painting, there is now one to be seen, greatest of all yet. . . . For boldness of outline, and delicacy of coloring, pictures taken in this manner rival all others." In 1855, F. A. Wenderoth of Philadelphia had introduced the American ivorytype, a paper print that was colored, sealed face down upon plate glass with hot wax, and backed with paper or cardboard before framing. This was different from the English ivorytype—John Mayall's process, patented in 1855—which was taken upon a sheet of artificial ivory.[6]

According to the *Daily Picayune* of February 20, 1861, Jacobs was in charge of the gallery at 93 Camp, while L. S. Lipman, who earlier had owned the gallery, was referred to

40. New Custom House, *ca.* 1860. Albumen photograph by Edward Jacobs.
Department of Archives and Manuscripts, Troy H. Middleton Library, Louisiana State University

as his "assistant." There Jacobs was offering all types of photographs, especially the life-size portrait, "colored with the same fidelity and effect as oil paintings." In his elegant galleries he featured photographs of celebrities, including one of Adelina Patti, the soprano who appeared at the French Opera House in November of 1860.

Besides Jacobs' and Edwards' galleries, Camille's Gallery advertised view photography in 1860. Camille's Gallery of Fine Art offered to take views of "Buildings, Mausoleums, Machinery, Engines, Steamboats, Farms, Landscapes, and Animals, dead or living." Their list ran the gamut of Victorian sensibilities, especially the picturesque. The stock views were additional to their varied services for architects and engineers, which included reproducing architectural plans and drawings "made to all scales." The United States Patent Office began using photography in 1860 to reproduce drawings.[7]

The promotion of the card stereograph accounted for an increasing production of paper images. First introduced in the United States about 1854, the card stereo was only mildly popular in New Orleans during the winter of 1859–1860 when Edwards had them to sell. B. Piffet's in December advertised "Stereoscopic—consisting of views of Paris, Spain, England and Ireland—also fine side [*sic*] views." F. and L. Piffet, another variety store, also offered stereoscopes and views of Europe and America. What may have been the first public exhibition of card stereographs in Louisiana was held at the industrial fair in Baton Rouge in March, 1860. This was one of the many stops for the London Stereoscopic Company's coast-to-coast tour of the states in that year. The Baton Rouge *Daily Gazette and Comet* of March 15, 1860, recommended them to readers. "STEREOSCOPIC VIEWS. In one of the rooms at the Barracks, and on the Fair ground, is a collection of views from the 'negatives' of the 'London Stereoscopic Company.' Scenes in the old world, of remarkable and interesting places, are thus brought home, just as painted in the sunlight of reality. Persons visiting the grounds, should take a look."[8] (At the same fair, New Orleans photographer John Clarke exhibited his own stereoscopic ambrotypes.) From 1860, the market for stereo view cards grew. Emulating the London Stereo Company, Anthony's of New York, the Langenheims of Philadelphia, and a few other eastern firms published their own series of American views. By 1866 there were numerous styles of viewers for sale and publishing firms in most large cities, including New Orleans.

Amidst the competition at the beginning of the decade, Anderson and Blessing made an impression with their magnificently appointed new gallery, which opened in November of 1859 at 61 Camp Street, across the street from the offices of the *Daily Picayune*. It was adorned with the "finest furniture, the most gorgeous products of the carpet loom, and superb specimens of art." There were numerous reception areas, workshops, offices, and a studio for the artists who finished the photographs in color. The firm employed a considerable number of operators and staff. Anderson and Blessing's gallery had all the styles to offer, but it was also reported that the gentlemen had "renewed the beautiful daguerrean art which fell into comparative desuetude in the first rage for ambrotypes and photographs . . . for the daguerreotype . . . is 'hard to beat.'"[9]

While dealing in a type of photography that was twenty years old, they were also prepared to offer the very latest, the *carte-de-visite*, "Photographs on Visiting Cards, by the hundred." Introduced in France in 1854, the *carte-de-visite* was a paper photograph made from a collodion negative and printed on albumenized paper. Usually measuring 2¼ by 3¾ inches, it was mounted on card stock not much larger, 2½ by 4 inches. Anderson and Blessing introduced them to New Orleans about the same time they appeared in the New York galleries. Within a year the new style was in great demand all over the country. *Humphrey's Journal* was obliged to offer instructions to its readership. "These portraits, as we shall call them—for they are indeed nothing more than full-length miniatures of the human face and form—are generally taken in a standing position, with a landscape background, or one made with panel paper, or a plain background having a small portion of a curtain in view. Some have a pedestal or a pillar or column represented with the subject resting the hand gracefully upon the one or the other. A chair somewhat ornamented, or a portion of a sofa, may be introduced with good effect" (41 and 42). To make these small photographs the *Journal* recommended using the stereoscopic camera with two tubes, because "by a new and beautiful arrangement of the box, an operator is enabled to produce four or more of these negatives upon one glass plate," thus making them inexpensive to produce in quantity.[10]

In March, 1860, Anderson and Blessing introduced the improved hallotype to New Orleans, calling its arrival "A New Era in Photography." According to the *Daily Picayune*, Anderson and Blessing for some months had been working

41. Young lady with column, *ca.* 1860. *Carte-de-visite* by William W. Washburn.
From the collections of the Louisiana State Museum

with the inventor, J. B. Hall, "in experimenting with an improved process of taking portraits." Hall came to New Orleans for a limited time to give personal supervision to the production of his pictures. The hallotype, patented in 1857, was one of the first variations on the collodion process. Like the ivorytype, it combined the qualities of the

42. Gentleman with top hat and cane, *ca.* 1860. *Carte-de-visite* by Theodore Lilienthal.
From the collections of the Louisiana State Museum

new paper prints with the familiar glass supports of the old ambrotype process. As described by Marcus A. Root, it consisted of "*combining* two or more pictures, which are facsimiles or duplicate impressions on semi-translucent material, so as to form one picture." The prints were made translucent with oil, cemented to glass with varnish, then placed in register one behind the other to give dimension to the image. It was said by *Humphrey's Journal* to have a stereoscopic relief, "which appears as though there was a *figure* placed behind the glass." It also commented that "since the introduction of Photography in this country, there has been nothing in the line of portraits so universally admired and highly esteemed by the public as this new style of pictures." In fact, by February of 1857 over three thousand had applied for rights to practice this process.[11]

Anderson and Blessing in 1860 had the exclusive right to manufacture hallotypes in New Orleans. The *Picayune* elaborated on the qualities of this *improved* hallotype. "By this new invention, likenesses may be secured at a nominal price, which possess a perfect ivory effect, and for delicacy of finish, natural roundness, and relief, and truthfulness of expression [are] equal to the finest and most costly ivory miniature. . . . It has been proved by various tests that neither heat, cold, dampness, water, the direct rays of the sun, nor the lapse of time mars the beauty, or dims the freshness of these very elegant pictures." Here was a new process that supposedly enabled an image to be made with the delicacy of tone found in a paper print, the durability of an ambrotype, and the relief of a daguerreotype, but without the reflective surface.

The photography business, as well as all other sectors of the city's economy, was faring agreeably well in 1860, but that situation abruptly changed with the political troubles of the winter and finally the secession of Louisiana from the Union in early 1861.

V
The Civil War Years

It was clear in late 1860 that America was on the brink of a disastrous war. The states were divided over many issues, the most burning of which was slavery. Further, the election of the Republican candidate, Abraham Lincoln, precipitated the inevitable. Louisiana's Governor Thomas Overton Moore, in early January, dispatched state troops to take over the United States Arsenal at Baton Rouge, as well as other Federal property. On January 26, 1861, the state severed its ties with the Union when delegates to a specially summoned convention signed the Ordinance of Secession. Louisiana joined the Confederacy on March 21. On the morning of April 12, southern forces under the command of General P. G. T. Beauregard, a native of Saint Bernard Parish, fired on Fort Sumter in the Charleston Harbor.

In the early months of 1861 dozens of military companies were formed throughout the state. They all came to the New Orleans area to train in camps established there and to be mustered into the Confederate army. The Metairie race course, where Edwards had recently photographed the horse races, was converted into a military camp.[1] As the *Daily Picayune* of May 26, 1861, described the city, "Considering that all thoughts are engrossed so entirely in the public affairs of the country, our city has worn an aspect of life and movement; our hotel registers show that travel is not utterly stopped, while our public haunts of all sorts evince the prevalence of the usual prosperity. The presence among us of such a large number of troops from the interior, and the busy preparation for departure on the part of so many of our own, make much stir, and impart to our streets an air of animation and gayety."

Several New Orleans photographers recorded Louisiana soldiers in their encampments. Among them was Mrs. E. Beachabard (or Beachbard), the only identified female gallery proprietor advertising in New Orleans at the time. She moved her operations to Camp Moore, situated north of Lake Pontchartrain in Tangipahoa Parish, and may have been the person described in the *Bee* of May 31, 1861, as "an enterprising ambrotype artist, who furnishes handsome warriors with their 'counterfeit presentments.'" The following November, Mrs. Beachabard was stricken with a fatal injury or illness and was buried at the camp.[2]

Twenty thousand men from the Crescent City alone were enrolled in the army. Between March 29 and April 11, several of their companies were sent to Pensacola, Florida, where the United States Navy Yard and forts guarding the bay had been held by Alabama and Florida troops since early January. J. D. Edwards, who had been at Pensacola periodically since January, recorded the New Orleans soldiers in camp and on drill: Louisiana Tigers in their exotic Zouave uniforms (43), Captain Charles Didier Dreux's Orleans Cadets, the Crescent Rifles, and the Chausseurs à Pied. At Fort Barrancas Edwards also photographed the interiors

43. Louisiana Tigers, Pensacola, Florida, 1861. Albumen photograph attributed to J. D. Edwards.
New Orleans Museum of Art

44. Rebel battery, Pensacola, Florida. Manning the guns along the beach at Warrington, 1861. Albumen photograph by J. D. Edwards.
Photo No. 77-HL-99-1, National Archives

and the barbette, with the men at their guns, copies of which were available in New Orleans by mid-May (44).[3]

According to Miller's *Photographic History of the Civil War*, Edwards pictured the "stirring scenes and opening tableaux of the war" and then became a spy for the Confederate secret service. He photographed the troops and guns of the Federal forces, including views of the Navy Yard, approaches to Forts Barrancas, McRae, and Pickens, and Union ships at close range. The allegation of Edwards' role is supported by the fact that his negatives were later seized in New Orleans by Union soldiers, and in May, 1862, a large cache of his photographs were seized in the Pensacola home of Stephen R. Mallory, Confederate secretary of the navy. Thirty to forty of Edwards' photographs, including the "spy prints," however, had been offered for sale in New Orleans newspapers in May, 1861: "War! War! Photo-

45. Cornelia Bach, *ca.* 1861. *Carte-de-visite* by Edward Jacobs.
From the collections of the Louisiana State Museum

graphic Views from the Seat of War."[4] A great demand existed for views of the war, as concern for the fate of the city grew more intense. On May 16, the *Bee* remarked that the views "give rather more satisfactory ideas of military affairs than can be derived from other sources. . . . Any of them will form an interesting souvenir for the parlor, particularly in the event considered now so near at hand of the capt[ure] of Fort Pickens."

Other photographers were also taking advantage of the prevailing anxieties. The *Daily Picayune* encouraged Jacobs' business by advising the following, "Every young man who

46. General P. G. T. Beauregard, *ca.* 1861. *Carte-de-visite* by John H. Clarke.
Collection of the late Marie Cruzat deVerges

goes to war ought, before starting, leave his likeness with his mother, sister, wife or other dear parent, and every lady whose husband, or brother, or son is sent to Pensacola, ought also to give her miniature to the gallant young volunteer; for, during the long night watch, or around the camp fire, it may be his only solace to look at the picture and kiss it." Such may have been the occasion for Cornelia Bach's photograph (45). Besides soliciting customers for the portrait trade, Jacobs also offered photographs of Generals Braxton Bragg, David E. Twiggs, and copies of the oil painting of General Beauregard by T. C. Healy, "so as to bring it within the reach of the public generally. . . . It will have an extensive circulation, beyond question."[5]

At his new gallery at 101 Canal Street, John H. Clarke sold *cartes* of Beauregard and photographed the Confederate soldiers, both young recruits and older veterans of former campaigns, as they enlisted in service (46 and 47).

47. Colonel Jean Jacques Alfred Alexander Mouton of Opelousas, *ca.* 1861. Quarter-plate ambrotype by John H. Clarke.
Courtesy of Mrs. Elemore Morgan, Sr.

Clarke also ventured out to photograph the rebel soldiers in their camps (48). At 46 Camp Street, the firm of B. and G. Moses offered *cartes* of the young Jefferson Davis, president of the Confederacy (49).

On May 26, 1861, the United States steamer *Brooklyn* blockaded the port of New Orleans, terminating the city's trade. For a year the city suffered from the effects; shortages of every commodity occurred and prices soared. With the blockade, too, photographers were cut off from their eastern suppliers and had to have their supplies smuggled in from the North. *Humphrey's Journal* noted that "the Photographic art down South has completely died out in consequence of the war. The miserable rebels are shut up like a rat in a hole." A photographer in New York City wrote to George

Smith Cook in Charleston in January of 1861: "Mr. Anthony tells me all his Southern trade is *dead*, but that his trade both North and West has but *very slightly fallen off*. Ditto Scovill. That is a bad sign. How do the Yancey's and Rhetts account for it? God save us all." Southern artists complained of "nothing to work with, and nobody to work for."[6]

Most New Orleanians, however, felt the conflict would be resolved soon and did little to fortify the city against a Union attack until the fall of 1861. According to one paper, the city assumed the aspect of a huge camp, and the "possibility of a wild attempt by the malevolent enemy to make a descent upon our coasts, or force his way up the river, is calling out the whole population to arms." Small industries were started to supply the troops with uniforms and weapons. Home brigades were organized, but the population of eligible men had already been drained. The city was ill pre-

48.Rebels' den, *ca.* 1861. Whole-plate ambrotype by John H. Clarke.
From the collections of the Louisiana State Museum

pared when "the Federal fleet that has so long been threatening this city, succeeded, yesterday morning, in passing the last line of our defence, notwithstanding a most gallant and vigorous resistance, at the fortifications below Chalmette. They took position in force in front of the city, which they now occupy, and sent on shore, under a flag of truce, two officers, who demanded an unconditional surrender."[7] Four days later, the city surrendered to Captain David G. Farragut. Although it was another year before the bastions at

49. Jefferson Davis, president of the Confederacy, *ca.* 1861. *Carte-de-visite* by Bernard and Gustave Moses.
Louisiana Historical Association Collection, Special Collections Division, Howard-Tilton Memorial Library, Tulane University

Vicksburg and Port Hudson fell, the course of the war in the West was determined when Farragut's men raised the Union flag over the South's largest city. New Orleans became the headquarters of Federal-occupied southern Louisiana, while a separate Confederate government was maintained in the central and northern sectors of the state. The Confederate capital was moved from Baton Rouge to Opelousas, and then in January, 1863, to Shreveport, where it survived until the end of the war.

After the surrender, New Orleans was placed under the command of General Benjamin F. Butler. While in charge of civilian affairs, from May until December, 1862, he instigated innumerable improvements. Butler organized relief agencies for the poor, repaired levees, which had been neglected since the blockade, and designed a drainage system to clear the streets of water and refuse, which were the breeding places of yellow fever. During the occupation there were no epidemics of yellow fever or any other serious disease. Butler's improvements, however, did not turn the opinion of the citizenry, who despised him. He was harsh with Confederate sympathizers; he closed newspapers, jailed editors, and expelled ministers from their pulpits. There were frequent clashes between the civilians and the Union soldiers. When he took command of the city, Butler had ordered all New Orleanians to sign an oath of allegiance to the United States. The Confiscation Act of 1862, passed by Congress that July, abetted Butler's intentions. Those who would not renounce their ties to the Confederacy had their homes, businesses, and other property seized.[8] The shops of artists and photographers were no exception. The studio of J. E. Mondelli, a portrait painter, was closed, and an oil portrait of Stonewall Jackson and "twenty-one other photographic likenesses of other rebel generals" were taken as contraband. Mondelli was arrested for painting the portrait, and two others were arrested for exhibiting it and the photographs.[9] In December, Butler was replaced by Nathaniel P. Banks, who remained as military governor until the spring of 1864.

With the decline of New Orleans' commerce, northern

speculators rushed to the city to set up businesses that thrived on wartime trade. Confederate money was worthless, but there were plenty of yankees present with United States currency to spend. Other outsiders bought up land from bankrupt planters, for it was practically worthless without slaves to work the fields.

With the intensification of the war in 1861 and 1862, several New Orleans photographers enlisted or were conscripted into service. J. H. Frobus, who owned his own ambrotype gallery in the late fifties and was also a "professor of art," held the rank of captain in a militia company. Theodore Lilienthal, who was associated with Joseph Kaiser in a daguerrean gallery in 1857 and 1858, enlisted with Jules Lilienthal as a cannoneer in the Washington Artillery. P. Camille served as a private in the French Brigade of the Louisiana Militia; A. Constant, who had his own ambrotype gallery in 1859, held the same rank in the Orleans Guards. William Guay was a second lieutenant in the militia. Samuel Moses enlisted as a private in the militia but was not active in combat because of his advanced age. His four sons also became soldiers: Gustave was commissioned a first lieutenant in the 21st Louisiana Infantry and was mustered out as a captain of the Army of Tennessee; Bernard was also commissioned a captain in the 21st Louisiana Infantry; Edward R. was a second lieutenant in the militia; and Louis was a private in the 1st Louisiana Militia.[10] How long Clarke remained in New Orleans during the early years of the war is not known. By 1864, he was in Texas serving as a purser with the Confederate army; in the following year he was in Mexico with the Mexican Foreign Legion.[11]

In May of 1862 the blockade was lifted and trade with the northern cities, via the Gulf of Mexico, gradually resumed. Large suppliers, the Anthony and Scovill companies, were once again able to ship their wares. Some New Orleans druggists offered the requisite chemicals to "Photographists" who had difficulty reestablishing connections with the northern supply houses.[12] The photographers who remained in the city worked under the restrictions imposed by a military occupation, but it was a situation that at the same time afforded them a new market, the Union officers and soldiers.

These portraits were made in all styles, some in daguerreotypes and ambrotypes, but mostly in tintypes and the new *cartes-de-visite*, which were small and could be easily sent in the mails. Like the miniatures, *cartes* became personal mementos of friends or loved ones, made more precious because of the war. Eliza Ripley of New Orleans described them as "gifts of near and dear friends, most of them with autograph attachments."[13] And because they could be easily mass produced by the use of the multilens cameras, many *cartes* were made of celebrities, including Confederate and Union generals. The photographic houses, especially Mathew Brady and C. D. Fredericks of New York, sold these by the thousands. Every photography gallery in New Orleans offered *cartes-de-visite* of the military heroes on both sides. Jacobs was offering portraits of Confederate heroes in early 1861, though in 1862 he catered to the Union trade as well. Jacobs photographed Farragut shortly after his victorious landing in New Orleans and his promotion to the rank of admiral on August 11. It is the image of a confident man (50). Before the Butlers departed in December Jacobs photographed Mrs. Butler in formal dress (51). Occasionally operators printed *cartes* that were political in nature. One anonymous New Orleans operator printed a lithograph that attacked the much-detested Butler (52).

The pirating of photographs, especially *cartes-de-visite* of celebrities, was an all too common practice. Lilienthal, who returned to his business in 1863, protected his own work by copyright. In September of that year he announced that he had applied for a copyright of his photographs of Nathaniel P. Banks and General Ulysses S. Grant and of Confederate Major General Franklin Gardner. At that time Lilienthal asked only moderate prices for his work, because of "the bad times where we are."[14]

In competition with the *carte-de-visite* in the 1860s was the melainotype, or tintype, which had been offered briefly in New Orleans in 1857 by William H. Abrams. (Apparently tintypes were not common in New Orleans until the

50. Admiral David G. Farragut, 1862. Albumen photograph by Edward Jacobs.
National Portrait Gallery, Smithsonian Institution

1860s.) When Anderson and Blessing advertised them in November of 1859, they were not called by the popular name but were described as "Ambrotypes taken on a new and improved plan upon metallic plates, thereby deviating the danger of breaking." The main advantage of the tintype was that it could be easily made, without the fuss of a negative, and like the *carte-de-visite*, sent in the mail. Though the tintype was referred to many times as "cheap looking," more soldiers posed during the Civil War for tintypes than for any other type of photograph.[15] Tintypes were made in various sizes, from the whole-plate size, such

51. Mrs. Benjamin F. Butler, 1862. *Carte-de-visite* by Edward Jacobs.
From the collections of the Louisiana State Museum

52. "Grand Federal Menagerie!! Now on Exhibition!!" *ca.* 1862. *Carte-de-visite* by unknown photographer.
From the collections of the Louisiana State Museum

as the tintype of the David R. Godwin family (53), to the one-sixth plate size tintype of Laure Beauregard, daughter of General Beauregard (54). They were nearly always placed in a case to resemble the daguerreotype or ambrotype or were slipped into a paper case the size of a *carte-de-visite*. Neither the daguerreotype nor the ambrotype was completely superseded by the tintype, though it survived them both in use.

Special albums for small tintypes and *cartes-de-visite* were manufactured and sold through the large eastern supply houses (55). These albums, which graced the tables of almost every Victorian parlor, contained the likenesses of rela-

53. David R. Godwin family, *ca.* 1861. Whole-plate tintype by Edward Jacobs.
From the collections of the Louisiana State Museum

54. Laure Beauregard, *ca.* 1863. Ninth-plate tintype by unknown photographer.
From the collections of the Louisiana State Museum

tives abroad and the young men off in battle, portraits of military heroes, views of battlefields, and sometimes the "fancies" (pretty young women, sentimental scenes, actors) tucked away on the last pages. In New Orleans albums were available by catalog from Anthony's in New York. On July 9, 1862, their advertisement appeared in the *Bee*. "Photographic Albums. We manufacture the most beautiful and durable that are made. CARD PHOTOGRAPHS of EMINENT AMERICANS for albums. Our assortment of this is ten-fold that of any other house. Catalogues sent on receipt of stamp. E. ANTHONY, 501 Broadway, New York, Manufacturer of Photographic Materials."

In 1863, a Republican administration was established in occupied Louisiana, with Michael Hahn, the labor candi-

55. *Carte-de-visite* album, with photographs of Alvina Godwin by Charles Marmu; and Dudley Calhoun of Amite, La., 1865, by unknown photographer.
From the collections of the Louisiana State Museum

date, elected as governor. The following year, a state constitution was devised which fell in line with the principles of the Reconstructionists, especially concerning the abolition of slavery. Yet "for more than a year after its adoption, Louisiana was under strict military rule and state government was but a pretense."[16] The state of the economy was extremely inflationary, with the prices of all goods very high.

From early 1864, the war was renewed in northern Louisiana. In April, General Banks moved against Shreveport, where Henry W. Allen sat as governor of Confederate Louisiana. Banks was defeated in his Red River campaign and was soon relieved of his military command by General Edward R. S. Canby. Canby was appointed head of the Military Division of the West Mississippi, including the Department of the Gulf and Arkansas. Banks was allowed to remain in charge of civilian affairs only.[17]

Many of the Confederate soldiers had volunteered for only one year. Like Lilienthal, William Guay and J. H. Frobus had returned from military service and were back in business by 1863. Guay photographed an unidentified

56. A Union officer, *ca.* 1865. *Carte-de-visite* by William Guay.
Photo No. 165-JT-387, National Archives

Union officer (56). He advertised his *cartes-de-visite* at $3 per dozen at his new gallery at 75 Camp Street in 1863. "Competition Outdone . . . Guay's Temple of Art." Frobus was in the employ of Washburn at his Canal Street gallery. Also in the early spring of 1863, Marmu, who had earlier worked with Picard, advertised his own Galerie de Portraits at 69 Royal Street, where he made a portrait of an unidentified priest (57).[18]

Anderson and Blessing dissolved their partnership in the fall of 1863, when Anderson assumed full interest in the gallery. Blessing established himself in a new shop at 24

57. A priest, *ca*. 1865. *Carte-de-visite* by Charles Marmu.
From the collections of the Louisiana State Museum

Chartres Street, where he offered photographic materials, published *cartes-de-visite* of celebrities, including Federal and Confederate generals, and views of the fortifications of Port Hudson, and engaged in the new photographic album trade.[19] Blessing's choice of this aspect of the business is reflected in a *Daily Picayune* article of March 13, 1864. "The 'Carte de Visite' has been so favorably received in all parts of the world that it has created a new branch of business, known as the photographic album trade. Mr. Blessing . . . has established himself in that trade, where can always be found albums of all sizes and qualities, which he offers at manufacturer's prices." Blessing was obviously giving competition to Anthony's. He was assured of rapid sales when in March of that same year he offered a miniature portrait of Marguerite Caroline Deslonde, the recently deceased wife of General Beauregard (58). Mrs. Beauregard was a member of

58. Marguerite Caroline Deslonde, 1864. *Carte-de-visite* by Samuel T. Blessing.
Mississippi Department of Archives and History

a prominent Louisiana family and wife of New Orleans' favorite military hero. At the same time, Blessing offered *carte-de-visite* views of New Orleans, which he published and sold at \$.25 each or \$2.50 per dozen (59).[20]

After Anderson worked alone for a year, he formed a partnership with Austin A. Turner in 1864. A native of North Carolina, Turner had had his own photographic gallery in New York City in 1855 and 1856 and again from 1862 to about 1866. He had received his first instruction from John Whipple in Boston, where in 1856 and 1857 he was in partnership with Cutting. At one time Turner was an operator for Mathew Brady and was later the supervisor for the publication of *cartes-de-visite* for D. Appleton and Company, a competitor of Anthony's in New York.[21]

59. The steamboat *New Era*, *ca.* 1865. *Carte-de-visite* published by Samuel T. Blessing.
Herman Cope Duncan and Family Papers, Department of Archives and Manuscripts, Troy H. Middleton Library, Louisiana State University

60. Ben Bridge, *ca.* 1864. *Carte-de-visite* by Samuel Anderson and A. A. Turner.
Louisiana Historical Association Collection, Special Collections Division, Howard-Tilton Memorial Library, Tulane University

Anderson and Turner improved the already celebrated saloon at 61 Camp Street with the addition of a second skylight, and offered the ivorytype as well as the hallotype, ambrotype, and paper photograph.[22] The firm did a large business in photographing veterans in uniform prior to their discharge from service. Their photograph of Ben Bridge (60), a member of the Washington Artillery, was mounted on Anderson's old card stock.

61. Anderson and Turner *carte-de-visite*, with revenue stamp, 1864.
Courtesy of Charles East

The photographic business nationally was very brisk during the spring of 1864, though it slackened considerably during the hot summer months. Everywhere materials were in short supply, and what was available was quite expensive due to the inflationary pressures of the war. In New Orleans, Blessing assured his customers that "notwithstanding the great rise in all merchandise," he was still selling photographs and albums at his "very lowest old prices." *Humphrey's Journal* anticipated a new call for troops, which "always makes the photograph business lively. . . . The fact that each one of our braves, before offering up his life on the altar of his country, has his picture taken, makes business for the operator, the stock dealer, and all others connected with them." But prospects for good business in the autumn were somewhat dimmed by the aggravation of a revenue tax imposed upon all photographs. The rate of taxation was determined by the retail price of the photograph; thus any additional retouching or coloring raised the tax. Photographs that sold for twenty-five cents or less required a stamp duty of two cents. *Cartes-de-visite* were usually included in this latter category, and the tax stamp was affixed to the back of the card (61).[23]

While operators in other southern cities such as Atlanta, Richmond, or nearby Baton Rouge necessarily concentrated on the war and its effects, in the occupied city of New Orleans, they were able to carry on a relatively lively practice in both portraiture and view photography. In addition to Blessing, William D. McPherson and his partner Mr. Oliver created a series of *carte-de-visite* views of the city and its monuments, buildings, parks, picturesque streets, and public squares, all of which captured the spirit of the city (62). McPherson and Oliver made many views in particular of the Vieux Carré and the American sector, thereby forming an

62. Jackson Square and Saint Louis Cathedral, *ca.* 1864. *Carte-de-visite* by McPherson and Oliver.
Marshall R. Dunham Album, Department of Archives and Manuscripts, Troy H. Middleton Library, Louisiana State University

important historical record of the appearance of the city at mid-century.

The wartime New Orleanian amused himself with simple diversions such as family outings and picnics. A photographer was occasionally invited along to take pictures. In November, 1863, Jacobs offered "Photographs of regimental pic-nic and family groups, etc., taken on short notice and in superior style." At that time Jacobs was associated with two partners, G. H. Brown and W. Ogilvie, experienced operators, in the National Art Union Photograph Gallery. They also offered views embracing every aspect of city life—"of public buildings, stores, family residences, steamboats and every description of water craft." In January of 1864 Jacobs appealed to Union loyalties with his spectacular portrait of General Banks and his entire staff, which was called "one of the largest and most successful group photographs ever taken in this city." That April the *Daily Picayune* complimented Jacobs for his dedication to photography and art by recollecting a stirring daguerreotype he had made during the devastating yellow fever epidemic in 1853. "A gentleman lay on the lounge, the death-bearing stream pouring from his mouth, while his five ministering friends stood anxious and attentive around his couch. Within a week four out of five were themselves in their graves, cast down by the same fell destroyer." Jacobs had made photographic copies of this pathetic scene.[24]

When the *Daily Picayune* announced on August 24, 1864 that Jacobs was retiring from the photography business, it was with a genuine expression of sorrow. With adulatory phrases the paper recounted Jacobs' long success in his profession and in the city, concluding, "There is not, we believe, in the whole United States, inclusive of the great cities of the North, a photographer who can do more than rival Mr. Jacobs in this branch of art. It is with unfeigned regret, therefore, that we notice his retirement." Jacobs had sold his establishment at 93 Camp Street to Gustave Moses, who had recently returned from military service, and Eugene Piffet. The new owners assumed all assets of the gallery, including the card stock, to which they added their

63. Moses & Piffet, successors to E. Jacobs, *ca.* 1865. *Carte-de-visite* stock.
Courtesy of Charles East

own names (63), and set to work making *carte-de-visite* portraits, such as that of a veteran of the Washington Artillery (64).

The wartime photographers who remain famous today, Mathew Brady, Timothy O'Sullivan, and Alexander Gardner, are remembered particularly for their views of military encampments, battlefields, and urban ruins. Several New Orleans photographers were also responsible for significant images of sites of southern campaigns. J. D. Edwards was in Pensacola from January through April, 1861. In the early months of 1863, McPherson and Oliver were taking pictures of the Union encampments at Baton Rouge, and in the late spring and summer of that year, they made a series of *carte-de-visite* views of the battlefield at nearby Port Hudson.[25] In 1864, they followed the progress of the war to Fort Morgan, Alabama, where they made a series of pictures

64. J. Howard Goodin, *ca.* 1864. *Carte-de-visite* by Gustave Moses and Eugene Piffet.
Louisiana Historical Association Collections, Special Collections Division, Howard-Tilton Memorial Library, Tulane University

of the ruined fort. These were large albumen prints (65 and 66) and *cartes-de-visite* (67), which the commanding officer of the United States Army Engineers, General Richard Delafield, sent to Washington, D.C., with his official report. McPherson and Oliver obtained a copyright for twenty-three views of Fort Morgan on October 1, 1864. The photographers also accompanied General Banks on his ill-fated Red River campaign in 1864 and photographed Admiral Farragut aboard the U.S. *Hartford*.[26] Gustave Moses and Eugene Piffet also worked in the service of the Union army, having been commissioned in the late summer

65. Interior of Fort Morgan from Bastion No. 2, 1864. Two albumen photographs forming a panoramic view, by McPherson and Oliver.
Photo No. 77-F-82-65, National Archives

66. Fort Morgan, Southeast Bastion, 1864. Albumen photograph by McPherson and Oliver.
Photo No. 77-F-82-69, National Archives

of 1864 by General Delafield to make a series of views of Fort Morgan and Mobile Point (68). Their work was sent to headquarters along with McPherson and Oliver's.[27]

It appeared that the Confederate cause in Louisiana was truly lost in the spring of 1865; President Davis had been captured in Georgia, and news of the April 9 surrender of General Robert E. Lee at Appomattox reached Louisiana six days later. The troops became demoralized and hundreds deserted. One-fifth of Louisiana's soldiers had died during the war; only Virginia, South Carolina, and Georgia had suffered more casualties. The plantations were overgrown and worthless for cultivation; and the state's old banks were insolvent. It has been estimated that one-half of the worth of Louisiana was lost as a result of the Civil War, wiping out the once-wealthy planter and New Orleans merchant alike.[28]

67. Interior of Fort Morgan, 1864. *Carte-de-visite* by McPherson and Oliver.
Photo No. 77-F-82-74½-11, National Archives

68. Mobile Point lighthouse, 1864. Albumen photograph by Gustave Moses and Eugene Piffet.
Photo No. 77-F-82-59, National Archives

VI
The Photographic Business in the Aftermath

In Louisiana the Civil War formally ended in the early summer of 1865, two months after Lee's capitulation at Appomattox, when the Confederate General Edmund Kirby Smith signed the articles of surrender on June 2 aboard the U.S. steamer *Fort Jackson* at Galveston, Texas. On June 10 the troops of the occupying United States Army arrived and enforced orders to free all slaves. Full trade reopened on the Red River and the Mississippi River, once again connecting New Orleans with the upper Mississippi and Ohio rivers. General Banks was relieved of his civilian duties, and General Philip H. Sheridan was placed in charge of West Louisiana. General Canby remained in charge of military affairs in the Division of the Gulf. Kirby Smith and other prominent Confederate leaders, including Governor Allen, soon afterward went into exile in Mexico.[1]

Military occupation of Louisiana continued for more than a decade. Many private buildings in New Orleans were confiscated for the use of the occupying army, and a few were photographed by an unidentified operator: General Canby's headquarters on Camp Street (69), the dispensary at the United States Army Barracks, known as Jackson Barracks (70), and the office of the New Orleans, Jackson and Great Northern Railroad Depot, which was on Calliope Street near the New Basin Canal. The depot (71) became the federal quartermaster's headquarters. Other views included the cavalry stables at Greenville and Sedgwick Hospital, both located in the present vicinity of Audubon Park, and the Odd Fellows Hall on Lafayette Square, which was used as a troop headquarters.[2]

Despite the presence of the soldiers, the city began to return to some degree of normalcy, as described by the editor of the 1866 *Gardner's New Orleans Directory*, the first published since 1861. "With the cessation of the war, commerce and civil industry have revived—our absent citizens have returned to their homes—our great storehouses are again the repositories of the chief articles of trade." The exports of cotton, sugar, and tobacco had risen slightly in the last two years of the war but would not return to the prewar volume. The production of sugar, for instance, as the war ended "was only a fraction of what it had been." And by 1865 the levees had deteriorated so much that floods threatened Louisiana agriculture throughout the Reconstruction years.[3]

69. General Canby's headquarters, Military Division of the Gulf, *ca.* 1865. Albumen print by unknown photographer.
Photo No. 165-C-889, National Archives

In addition to great material losses, New Orleans under the so-called Reconstruction became an arena for the political struggle between the radical Republicans and the conservative Democrats. If the Louisianian had indeed accepted defeat and the emancipation of the slaves, "he did not repent of secession, and he would not accept the Negro as an equal politically, socially, or otherwise." Radical Republicans, who supported the movement for Negro rights, constantly battled with conservative factions of the old guard for control of the government, leading to violent incidents like the bloody riot in July, 1866, in which three white and thirty-four black Unionists were killed and numerous others

70. U.S. barracks, dispensary, *ca.* 1865. Albumen print by unknown photographer.
Photo No. 165-C-884. National Archives

71. Jackson Railroad building, used for offices of headquarters, Quarter Master Department, *ca.* 1865. Albumen print by unknown photographer.
Photo No. 165-C-880, National Archives.

wounded. There was much discussion and many disparate accounts of the riot, causing one paper to state, "If Turner and Cohen could have brought their photography to bear on the riot of the 30th July there would have been little chance for the itinerant dealers in loyalty to misrepresent its occurrences."[4]

A succession of men served in political offices at the behest of the Republicans. Many of them were not from Louisiana, nor indeed the South. "Native white southerners and Negroes were to be found in positions of power in Louisiana throughout Radical Reconstruction, but the outstanding figures were men from outside the South, most of them Union army veterans who had known Louisiana during the war. Some were idealists, some were dutiful servants of the national Republican party, many were opportunists, and entirely too many were shamelessly corrupt." Political and financial difficulties were compounded by destructive acts of nature. The deterioration of the levees caused disastrous floods in 1866 and 1867, and in the latter year New Orleans was visited by the "saffron scourge," the first epidemic since Butler had ordered the city cleaned up. The pestilence not only delayed the city's "business season" for at least two months but also killed approximately three thousand persons.[5]

In spite of the postwar struggles for political power and the trials of rebuilding, the citizens of New Orleans did not abandon their interest and participation in the social and cultural events in the city. Theater, opera, balls, and varied exhibitions, which were still enjoyed during the Union occupation, continued throughout the Reconstruction period. And having one's likeness made by a photographer remained an important event for both the civilian and the soldier, and even for the grand Creole gentleman, Bernard de Marigny, whose fabulous life paralleled the golden era of New Orleans (72).

As *Humphrey's Journal* had so aptly put it, "A call for troops always makes the photograph business lively," and indeed this was also the case when the soldier prepared himself for the transition to civilian life. In the summer of 1865 hundreds of soldiers, both Union and Confederate, posed for their last portrait in uniform. As the soldier returned, so did the photographer. In reference to its southern subscribers the *Journal* commented, "We are surprised on looking over our lists to notice how many of our Southern friends have found their way back to us. We had supposed that most all of them had been scattered by the ravages of war to the four quarters of the Union; but no; there they are, the same old familiar names at the same old post office! If they got scattered by the war, it is certain that hundreds of them have found their way home again!"[6]

In New Orleans, some photographic firms like Blessing's remained in business for the duration of the war, but many more were reopened after their owners returned home, and several new businesses were begun. The annual state fairs

72. Bernard de Marigny, *ca.* 1865. *Carte-de-visite* by unknown photographer.
Historic New Orleans Collection

that had offered local photographers an opportunity to exhibit examples of their work were resumed after the war. Whereas the fairs of the 1840s and 1850s had been held in Baton Rouge, the site of the new series of fairs, sponsored by the Mechanics' and Agricultural Fair Association of

Louisiana, was in New Orleans. The First Annual Grand Fair was held from November 20 to 27, 1866. The fair represented Louisiana's efforts to rebuild; displays of machinery, agricultural products, and varied objects such as photographs, attested to the spirit not only to survive but to achieve, in spite of the disruption and destruction of the war. And as the *Daily Picayune* commented, "The absorbing interest which is taken in the FAIR is one of the signs that the popular mind is withdrawing itself from the absorbing attention hitherto given to political affairs, and turning to the practical pursuits of life." The competition of the fairs reflected and encouraged the use of novel and varied styles of photography. Prizes were awarded in such categories as best photograph in oil, best photograph in watercolor, best plain photograph, best series of stereoscopic views, best set of views of public buildings, best views of landscapes, best specimens on ivory.[7]

The *Duncan & Co.'s New Orleans Business Directory* for 1865 listed about twenty-five photographers or photographic firms, several of the names familiar and many of them new. Samuel T. Blessing's large photographic supply store on Chartres Street sold *cartes-de-visite* and albums. At the close of the war, Blessing advertised a large assortment of *cartes* including likenesses of all the Confederate generals for sale by the hundreds or thousands.[8] Blessing, like other local firms, stocked views as well, but he became a large publisher of stereo views only after the war, following the example of the New York firm of E. and H. T. Anthony, who had inaugurated their own stereo view series in 1859.[9]

Among Blessing's early offerings was a series of views dramatizing the growth of the city. A view looking westward, with Saint Patrick's Church on Camp Street in the foreground, was one of eight views that formed a panoramic sweep of New Orleans (73). Blessing also published views of buildings, monuments, and cemeteries, including one of Saint Louis Cemetery No. 2 (74). Whether Blessing's operators actually took the photographs he published is not known, but he seems to have been primarily a publisher and his firm a photographic materials depot following the termi-

73. Panorama of New Orleans No. 413, *ca.* 1866. Stereo view published by S. T. Blessing.
From the collections of the Louisiana State Museum

74. Saint Louis Cemetery No. 2, *ca.* 1866. Stereo view published by S. T. Blessing.
From the collections of the Louisiana State Museum

75. Dr. Clapp's church, *ca.* 1866. Stereo view published by Theodore Lilienthal.
From the collections of the Louisiana State Museum

nation of his partnership with Anderson in 1863. Although Blessing frequently published views made by other photographers without acknowledging the maker, he remained a prominent figure in the photographic business in New Orleans for three decades after the Civil War.[10]

Theodore Lilienthal, who during the war years was active in the military *carte-de-visite* trade, also became a publisher and maker of stereo views of New Orleans. His views covered a geographic range of the city from Canal Street to Carrollton, then a rural retreat above the city. In 1866, the year he was joined in the business by his brother Louis, Theodore also produced a series of stereo views of the city, constituting a panorama taken from the steeple of Saint Patrick's church; the view of Dr. Theodore Clapp's Church was part of that series (75). Clapp, the founder of the First Congregational Unitarian Church, was a popular clergyman in New Orleans for over thirty years. A stereo view of a Mardi Gras parade rounding the corner of Canal and Saint Charles streets (76) and a view of Saint Charles Street from Canal Street (77) were two other early publications of his

76. Mardi Gras parade, *ca*. 1866. Stereo view published by Theodore Lilienthal.
From the collections of the Louisiana State Museum

77. Statue of Henry Clay, corner of Saint Charles and Canal streets, *ca*. 1866. Stereo view published by Theodore Lilienthal.
From the collections of the Louisiana State Museum

firm. Like most firms, Lilienthal's also made large albumen prints of monuments and buildings in the city; his picture of Mallard's famous furniture emporium at the corner of Royal and Bienville streets was made about 1867 (78). Eighteen sixty-six was the year certain American photographers began issuing various series of card stereographs, independent of the larger publishers such as Anthony; and in New Orleans Lilienthal seems to have been one of the earliest publishers of his own stereo views.[11] Before the end of the decade virtually every gallery owner advertised stereo views made from original negatives or purchased from other publishers.

In addition to consistently winning awards at the annual state fairs for his landscape and urban photography and his series of stereoscopic views, Theodore Lilienthal received international recognition and a bronze medal for his views at the 1867 Paris Universal Exposition. By 1885 Lilienthal had become also a manufacturer of picture frames and in that year was preparing to send specimens of his work to the 1889 World's Fair.[12]

Samuel Anderson, Blessing's former partner, advertised separately from Austin A. Turner in 1865, announcing in August that he was alone in the business and had just returned from the North with all the latest improvements. He reopened his gallery at 61 Camp Street. Anderson, like Lilienthal, also participated in the First Annual Grand Fair, where his photograph of Jacob Barker, a local attorney and merchant, was very much admired, and where he received a "diploma" for the best photograph colored in oil and a citation for the best picture colored in India ink.[13]

Turner, meanwhile, in March of 1865, opened the New Orleans Photographic Company, where he took the portrait of an unidentified lieutenant colonel (79). The *Daily Picayune* wrote of the gallery opening: "We learn that we are to have a new photographic establishment, at 57 Camp street that promises to far excel any now in the city. . . . We shall expect to see superior pictures from this house." The gallery was short-lived; in July of 1866 Turner formed a business association with Warren M. Cohen but retained the same address at 57 Camp Street. On September 19 of that year

78. P. Mallard, Fine Furniture, *ca.* 1867. Albumen photograph by Theodore Lilienthal.
Martha Ann and Ray Samuel Collection

Turner died, leaving his interest in the gallery to Cohen. At the time of Turner's death the business had liabilities of $4,515.34, complicated by Turner's having left *two* widows.[14] The next month Cohen announced, "This Gallery is open and will be carried on the same as usual." In that same month the firm received praise for some of their *cartes-de-visite*. "The pictures are exceedingly fresh looking, and in

79. A lieutenant colonel of the Confederate army, *ca.* 1865. *Carte-de-visite* by the New Orleans Photographic Company (A. A. Turner).
Courtesy of Anne Tucker

some instances the flesh tints are almost equal to painting. Among the number received we recognize the faces of some of the actors and actresses now performing in New Orleans." The firm of Turner and Cohen received a "diploma" for the best photograph in watercolor at the Annual Grand Fair of 1866. Cohen continued to advertise in New Orleans at least until late in 1867.[15]

William W. Washburn not only resumed his photographic gallery business after the war but remained at his Canal Street address for fifty years, becoming one of the outstanding portrait photographers in the city. Specializing in unadorned paper prints, his specimens received the prize for best plain photograph in the fairs of 1866 and 1868. At the

80. General J. L. Lewis, *ca.* 1865. *Carte-de-visite* by A. Constant.
From the collections of the Louisiana State Museum

time of his death in 1903 Washburn had earned the sobriquet Dean of New Orleans Photography.[16]

Washburn had serious competition, however, from both Lilienthal and John H. Clarke, who reopened his gallery at 101 Canal Street in 1868. Clarke continued his superior work in portraiture, specializing in photographs of children, until his retirement in 1900. He died in the city fourteen years later. At Numbers 20 and 21 Hospital Street in the Vieux Carré, A. Constant reopened his gallery of portraiture and photography, where he made the *carte-de-visite* portrait of General J. L. Lewis (80).

Gustave Moses, who in 1864 had been in business with Eugene Piffet, went to Saint Louis to photograph Union soldiers as they returned to civilian life. He then came back to New Orleans, where he became a partner once again with his brother Bernard, whose talents as a portrait painter

81. A young couple, *ca.* 1865. *Carte-de-visite* by Bernard and Gustave Moses.
Courtesy of Charles East

EPISODE OF THE AMERICAN WAR.
Determination and courage of a Confederate prisoner at Vicksburg.

82. *Episode of the American War*, 1864. Albumen photograph by Bernard and Gustave Moses.
From the collections of the Louisiana State Museum

added another dimension of professionalism to the firm. Perhaps because of Bernard, the firm specialized in the portrait trade (81).

With the Moses brothers, both Confederate veterans, antifederal sentiment was strong. Shortly after the reinstitution of the firm, B. and G. Moses, the two copied the painting by local artist Dominique Canova that described the plight of one P. Albert Melton. When a prisoner of the Union army at Vicksburg, Mississippi, Melton had cut off his left hand in defiance of his captors. The full story, which was included on the photographic print (82), had been published in the New Orleans *Bee*, December 4, 1864.

> Vicksburg, Nov. 29th. Among the prisoners captured in Louisiana by the United States Gunboats, and who had up

> to this date been closely confined was one P. Albert Melton, a man noted for his daring and resolute character. This morning he was ordered to go to work with the other prisoners and upon his refusal, the guard was sent for to enforce obedience, when suddenly seizing upon a hatchet he chopped off his left hand, not however by a single blow but by repeated strokes,—then presenting the stump to the Lt. on duty he cooly asked him if he thought he should not work for the government of the United States.

The sensational painting had become famous in the city, and the Moses brothers took the opportunity to realize both political and financial satisfaction from the distribution of prints. This print was among the war memorabilia that was displayed in Confederate homes, along with portraits of Generals Lee and Beauregard and President Davis. Gustave Moses' firm, later G. Moses and Sons, survived into the 1930s.[17]

William Guay made *cartes-de-visite* (83) and distinguished himself with certificates for best colored photographs on porcelain and best plain photograph on porcelain at the 1868 fair. The next year Guay was associated in New York with the notorious William Mumler of Boston, who caused scandals and lawsuits with the practice and promotion of spirit photography, an early profitable use of trick photography.[18]

Some photographers of Civil War views, like J. D. Edwards, did not return to New Orleans. Edwards was in Virginia for a time and then settled in Atlanta in 1886. He was the partner of Lewis K. Dorman until 1887, when his son joined him in the business. Edwards died in that city fourteen years later.[19]

McPherson and Oliver, also well known for their Civil War views, chose to come back to New Orleans at the closing of the war and opened a gallery in 1864. But then in 1865 McPherson had a photographic studio of his own, where he made *cartes-de-visite*, both portraits (84) and views of the city (85 and 86). McPherson operated his studio at 132 Canal Street until his death in October, 1867. The contents of his studio, including the traditional props of the

83. Father and son, *ca*. 1867. *Carte-de-visite* by William Guay.
From the collections of the Louisiana State Museum

business—one wooden column, one wooden railing, and one high stool—were sold at public auction. His collection of negatives was also sold.[20] The administrator of McPherson's estate was none other than Blessing, who may

84. Gray Doswell, 1867. *Carte-de-visite* by W. D. McPherson.
From the collections of the Louisiana State Museum

85. Orleans Parish Prison, *ca.* 1866. *Carte-de-visite* by W. D. McPherson.
From the collections of the Louisiana State Museum

86. City Park, *ca.* 1866. *Carte-de-visite* by W. D. McPherson.
From the collections of the Louisiana State Museum

very likely have employed McPherson's negatives in his publishing business. McPherson's works may have been purchased by other local photographers as well (the use of at least one print has been noted). The Irish-born photographer, Louis Issac Prince, copied a McPherson print that he may have purchased from the estate or pirated before McPherson's death.

Prince, who had been on the roll of prisoners of war and paroled in 1865, was one of several new photographers who opened businesses in New Orleans. He died two weeks after McPherson, however, perhaps from the yellow fever epidemic that beleaguered the city in 1867. The indebtedness of Prince's estate lends insight into the operation of small galleries and their dependence on others. According to court records, Prince owed Anderson a large amount for supplies, Washburn for coloring photographs, and three photographers, J. A. Sheldon, S. Robira, and J. J. Comeaux, for services.[21]

Although the economy was depressed, several operators besides Prince found sufficient business to locate perma-

87. Canal Street at the corner of Camp Street, *ca.* 1866. Stereo view by W. H. Leeson.
Louisiana Division, New Orleans Public Library

88. New Basin Canal, *ca.* 1866. Stereo view by W. H. Leeson.
Louisiana Division, New Orleans Public Library

nently in the Crescent City. Among them were J. W. Petty, W. H. Leeson, and M. J. Hinton, who named his gallery the Crescent Photography Gallery. Leeson, who worked in New Orleans throughout the decade, outfitted himself with a wagon that enbled him to travel to outlying areas to make views. He also made views within the city, such as one of Canal Street at the corner of Camp (87) and a more tranquil scene at the New Basin Canal (88). He advertised as a "Photographer and publisher of Stereoscopic Views of New Orleans and Vicinity."[22]

Adrian Persac, an artist who had been associated with William Vail as a photographer in Baton Rouge ten years earlier, in 1865 advertised in New Orleans with a new partner, a Mr. Legras. They offered "de toutes sortes de Photographie." Then in 1866 Persac announced he was alone in the business; but like Jules Lion before him, Persac chose to concentrate not on photography but on drawing and painting, to which in addition to architecture he soon devoted himself entirely.[23]

Lion died in 1866, the year that marked the beginning of a new style among photographers, the cabinet card. This style was hailed as a means of stimulating the industry by Edward L. Wilson, an editor of a popular new photography journal and the leading spokesman for the art in the last half of the century. "Something must be done to create a new and greater demand for photographs. Photographers in all directions are complaining that trade is dull. The *carte-de-visite* . . . seems to have grown out of fashion. Everyone is surfeited with them. . . . The Adoption of a new size is what is wanted. . . . A new size, called the cabinet card, has just been adopted in England."[24]

By November of 1866, one month after Wilson's declaration, the cabinet card was being made in New York; E. and H. T. Anthony immediately began manufacturing albums for them.[25] The cabinet card was subsequently adopted in cities throughout the United States, and in New Orleans it became the specialty of photographers like Robira, the Daliet brothers, Clarke, and Washburn. The cabinet card was a paper print approximately 4 inches by 5½ inches, mounted on a card 4½ inches by 6½ inches. It was intended to, and did finally, replace the smaller *carte-de-visite*, not only because of its size but also because of its more elaborate style. With its unusually rich assortment of props creating a lush Victorian interior or a quaint rustic "exterior" scene, the theatrical backdrop of the cabinet card contrasted sharply with the simple single chair and Doric column that had formed the background of earlier images. Photography had come a long way from the daguerreotype, which was obsolete in the 1860s, with its long exposure and unique image, to the quickly made and easily reproduced cabinet card. Soon the camera, once restricted to the domain of artists and professionals, would be in the hands of the amateur.

In New Orleans it had begun in 1840, literally with one man, Jules Lion, and by the end of the 1860s, photography was a business producing thousands of photographs that continued to record the unique nature of the Crescent City and her people.

Biographical Checklist of New Orleans Photographers

This checklist includes those photographers who worked in New Orleans during the period 1840 to 1870. In looking at this information the reader should take into consideration the following: First, a city directory date usually means that the photographer was there late in the previous year when information for the directory was generally gathered; and second, street numbers were frequently changed, and thus a photographer could have remained in his same studio or gallery, even though the directory indicates a number change from the year before. Sometimes two different directories for the same year will list two different addresses for a photographer. When this occurs, a slash mark will indicate the discrepancy. Publishing information for books listed in the sources following the biographies will be found in the bibliography.

Abbreviations

L'Abeille	*L'Abeille de la Nouvelle-Orléans*
Bee	New Orleans *Bee*
Booth	Andrew Booth, *Records of Louisiana Confederate Soldiers and Louisiana Confederate Commands*
BD	Business Directory (as listed by individual titles in the Bibliography)
Cemetery Records	Records in the Louisiana State Museum Library for New Orleans Cemeteries
Census (1850, 1860)	United States Census Records for New Orleans
CD	New Orleans City Directory (as listed by individual titles in the Bibliography)
c.	Corner
DJ	*Daguerreian Journal*
HJ	*Humphrey's Journal*

LSM	Louisiana State Museum
MD	*New Orleans Merchants' Diary and Guide*, 1857 and 1858
Newhall	Beaumont Newhall, *The Daguerreotype in America*
NOPL	New Orleans Public Library
PAJ	*Photographic Art-Journal* and *Photographic and Fine-Art Journal*
Rinhart	Floyd Rinhart and Marion Rinhart, *American Daguerreian Art*
Root	Marcus A. Root, *The Camera and the Pencil*
Succ. Records	New Orleans Court Succession Records
Welling	William Welling, *Collectors' Guide to Nineteenth-Century Photographs*

Abrams, William H. *MD*, 1857–58: proprietor, ambrotype, daguerreotype, photograph, melainotype, and portrait painting saloon, 74 Chartres St. CD, 1860, 1861: daguerrean, 150 Royal St.

Anderson, Peter S. CD, 1868–69: photographer, 157 Poydras St. CD, 1870: photographer.

Anderson, Samuel Born in Pennsylvania. December, 1856: partner of Samuel T. Blessing, successors to W. W. Washburn, 120 Canal St.; another gallery at Tremont St., Galveston, Tex.; sold daguerreotypes, ambrotypes, paper photographs. 1857: firm moved to 134 Canal St.; tintypes offered. 1859: moved to 61 Camp St.: advertised solar camera process. 1860: advertised hallotypes; J. B. Hall visited. Fall, 1863: dissolution of partnership; bought out Blessing. 1864: associated with Austin A. Turner, 61 Camp St. August, 1865: Anderson alone. 1866: received award, best photograph in oil, Grand Fair, N.O. CD, 1868: partner of J. H. Clarke, 183 Canal St. CD, 1869, 1870: alone at 183 Canal. 1869: won bronze medal, best photograph on ivory, Grand Fair. (*Daily Picayune*, December 2, 1856; *The Industries of Houston*, [Houston: 1887]; *Daily Picayune*, October 30, 1859; March 16, 25, 1860; September 11, November 1, 1863; November 8, 19, 1864; August 11, 1865; Reports of the Grand Fairs, 1866, 1869)

Andrews, James 1860 Census: born *ca.* 1830 in Georgia; died July 18, 1863, in N.O. CD, 1856: daguerrean, 3 St. Charles St. 1856: partner of Bennett in National Daguerreotype and Photograph Gallery, 3 and 8 St. Charles. *MD* 1857–58: at 5 and 8 St. Charles. CD,

1858: 3 St. Charles. CD, 1859: at 2 and 8 St. Charles. CD, 1860: ambrotypist, 8 St. Charles.
(*Daily Picayune*, July 19, 1863; *New Delta*, March 23, 1856)

Anson, Edward CD, 1858: at 3 St. Charles St. [Andrews' photographic establishment]. CD, 1860: photographer, 239 Thalia St.

Arsane, Ben 1860 Census: born *ca.* 1845 in France; 1860: ambrotypist.

Bader, John W. CD, 1867, 1868: photographer, 201 Tchoupitoulas St.

Ball, Lyons & Co. CD, 1869: photographic supplies, 42 and 44 Camp St.

Baltar, Jacinto CD, 1858: ambrotypist, 17 Victory St. CD, 1859, 1860: at 233 Orleans. During war: Pvt., European Brig., Spanish Regt., La. Militia. BD 1865: at coffeehouse.
(Booth, Vol. I, p. 113)

Bancker, J. C. CD, 1867: ambrotypist, 120 Elysian Fields.

Barker, B. 1860 Census: born *ca.* 1831 in Massachusetts; 1860: photographer

Barry, G. 1843: daguerrean, 3 St. Charles St.; "pupil of Daguerre"; offered miniature daguerreotype portraits.
(*Daily Picayune*, January 15, 1843)

Beachabard, Mrs. E.[Beachbard] CD, 1860: proprietor, ambrotype saloon, 203 Rampart St. CD, 1861: at 173 Rampart. Died November 22, 1861, at Camp Moore, La.
(Charles East to Mary Louise Tucker, January 9, 1980)

Bennett, —— [John A. ?] 1856: partner of James Andrews in National Daguerreotype and Photographic Gallery, 3 and 8 St. Charles St.
(*New Delta*, March 23, 1856)

Bishop, T. B. CD, 1868: photographic gallery, 142 Canal St.

Blanc, J. P. CD, 1861: photographer, 32 St. Philip St.

Blanks, A. CD, 1867: photographer, 113 Canal St.

Blessing, Samuel T. 1860 Census: born *ca.* 1832 in Maryland; died November 18, 1897, in St. Louis. 1856–1863: partner of Samuel Anderson. Fall, 1863: dissolution of partnership. 1863–69: photographic supplies company, wholesale and retail; published stereo views of N.O., 24 Chartres St.
(*Times-Democrat*, November 19, 1897; CD, 1857–61, 1866–70; *Daily Picayune*, September 11, November 8, 1863)

Bonnemer, —— CD, 1866: photographer, with Victor Mary, 96 Chartres St.

Boucher, F. CD, 1850: daguerrean, 52 St. Charles St.

Bouny, Louis J. CD, 1870: photographer.

Bourges, A. CD, 1859: daguerrean, St. Anthony St. near Prosper St. CD, 1860: at 211 Villere.

Boutevillain, H. CD, 1867: photographer, 128 Bourbon St.

Brown & Co., C. CD, 1842: daguerreotype portrait painter, 195 Chartres St. January, 1842: offered daguerreotype miniature portraits, 165 Chartres.
(*Commercial Bulletin*, January 26, 1842)

Brown, George Hay 1863: partner of Edward Jacobs, Walter Ogilvie, at National Art Union Photograph Gallery, 93 Camp St.
(*Daily Picayune*, November 1, 1863)

Burnham, E. R. CD, 1868: photographic operator at W. H. Leeson's, 167 Poydras St.

Byron, Calvin BD 1865: photographer, 69 Canal St.

Calatrabe, Eugene CD, 1868: photographer, Customhouse St.

Camille, P. 1860 Census: born *ca.* 1832 in France. CD, 1858, 1859: daguerrean, 18 Hospital St. and 108 Old Levee St. CD, 1860, 1861: at Gallery of Fine Art, Old Levee c. Hospital. BD, 1865: at 19 Hospital.

Cardido, Jose *MD*, 1857–58: daguerrean, 15 Victory.

Carpenter, Thomas H. BD, 1865, CD, 1866: photographer, Baronne St. c. Poydras St. CD, 1867: photographer, 538 Magazine St.

Carr, R. CD, 1846: daguerrean, 74 Royal St.

Censier, Louis [Cencier] 1860 Census: born *ca.* 1839 in Louisiana. CD, 1858: daguerrean, 259 Burgundy St. CD, 1859: at 142 Toulouse St. CD, 1860: daguerrean, Old Levee St. c. Hospital St. [Camille's Gallery of Fine Art?]. CD, 1866, 1867: photographer, 44 Hospital.

Chase, —— 1843: daguerrean, 44 Canal St.
(*Courier*, April 10, 1843)

Clarke, John Hawley [Clark] 1860 Census: born *ca.* 1831 in Delaware; died July 16, 1914, in N.O. *Washiington and Georgetown Directory*, 1853: with Marcus A. Root in daguerreotype gallery, Pennsylvania Ave., Washington, D.C. 1856: with F. S. Hedrick, 94 Canal St., in N.O. 1858, proprietor, gallery at 94 Canal St. CD, 1860: proprietor, photographic gallery, 99 Canal. 1860: exhibited plain and colored photographs, stereoscopic ambrotypes, Baton Rouge fair. CD, 1861: at 101 Canal. 1864: purser in Confederate Army, Tex. 1865: expedition with Mexican Foreign Legion. CD, 1868:

partner with S. Anderson. CD, 1869: proprietor, photographic saloon, 101 Canal. CD, 1870: at 101 Canal St.
(Orleans Parish Death Records, NOPL; Root, p. 366; *Daily Orleanian*, December 21, 1856; *PAJ*, XI [August, 1858], 244; *Sugar Planter*, March 24, 1860; Accession record 6705, LSM; verso of photograph, LSM.)

Cohen, Warren A. 1862: Pvt., Crescent Regt., La. Infantry. July, 1866: partner of Austin A. Turner, 57 Camp St.; received award, best photograph in water colors, Grand Fair, N.O. CD, 1867, 1868: proprietor, photograph gallery, 57 Camp.
(Booth, Vol. II, p. 372; *Daily Picayune*, July 7, 1866; *Report of the First Annual Grand Fair*)

Constant, A. [Anton?] 1853: living in N.O. BD, 1858–59: proprietor, ambrotype saloon, 17 Hospital St. CD, 1859: at Hospital c. Old Levee St. CD, 1860: ambrotypist, 26 Hospital. CD, 1861: proprietor, A. Constant & Co., portrait painters, artists, and photographers, 20 and 23 Hospital. November, 1860: at 20–21 Hospital. CD, 1861, BD, 1865: 20–21 Hospital. CD, 1866: with Louis Moses, 21 Hospital St. CD, 1867: A. Constant and Moses, 21/30 Hospital. CD, 1868–70: photographer, 21 Hospital.
(Ship Passenger Lists, NOPL; *L'Abeille*, November 15, 1860)

Cook, George Smith Born 1819, Stratford, Conn.; died 1902, near Richmond, Va. 1838: traveled South. *ca.* 1843: painter in N.O. *ca.* 1844: daguerrean in N.O. 1845: left N.O., taught daguerreotyping in South. 1849: in Charleston, S.C. 1851: operator for Mathew Brady. 1852–75; daguerrean in Charleston. 1873: settled in Richmond, Va.
(Rinhart, 115; Kocher and Dearstyne, *Shadows in Silver*, 6; *PAJ*, I [May, 1851], 285.)

Cornet, Felix 1860 Census: born *ca.* 1834 in Louisiana; 1860: ambrotypist in N.O.

Cornog, A. W. CD, 1867: photographer, 75 Camp St. CD, 1869: photographer.

Cornu, F. CD, 1858: daguerrean, 304 St. Claude St. CD, 1859: at Bayou Rd. CD, 1860: at 306 Bayou Rd. During war: Pvt., 1st Chausseurs-à-pied, La. Militia.
(Booth, Vol. II, p. 446)

Costanzi, F. E. 1858: proprietor, photography and ambrotype gallery, 11 Camp St. CD, 1861: photograph gallery, 66 Bienville St. 1862: 2nd Lt., La. Militia.
(*Bee*, December 29, 1858; Booth, II, 449)

Curry, William CD, 1867, 1868: photographer, 72 Spain St.

Curtright, —— 1850: studio in Baton Rouge; previously at 28 Camp St., N.O. (*Gazette*, September 21, 1850)

Cuslauyi, P. 1860 Census: born *ca.* 1829 in N.O.; 1860: photographer in N.O.

Daliet, Aristide CD, 1869: photographer, 35 Frenchman St. CD, 1870: at 33 Frenchman.

Daliet, Jules 1861: Pvt., 4th La. Infantry. 1863: on Confederate army rolls. 1864: prisoner of war. May, 1865: released on Oath of Allegiance to U.S. CD, 1869: photographer, 35 Frenchman St. CD, 1870: at 33 Frenchman [A. Daliet's].
(Booth, Vol. II, p. 524)

Daliet, Octave CD, 1869: at picture gallery, 35 Frenchman St. CD, 1870: photographer, 33 Frenchman [A. Daliet's].

Damarast, August 1860 Census: born *ca.* 1818 in Louisiana; 1860: ambrotypist in N.O.

Dauboin, G. CD, 1850: watchmaker and jeweler in N.O. CD, 1854: daguerrean, Tchoupitoulas St. near Jackson St. CD, 1855: at Magazine St. near St. Andrew St. CD, 1857; watchmaker. BD, 1858: at daguerreotype gallery, Magazine near St. Andrew. CD, 1859–61, jeweler.

David, Louis P. 1850 Census: born *ca.* 1808 in Cuba. CD, 1841–49; sign and ornamental painter, portrait painter in N.O. CD, 1850–54: portrait painter, drawing master, daguerreotypist, 80 Royal St. CD, 1855, 1856: daguerrean, 71 Bienville St. CD, 1857–59: at 152 Royal. CD, 1860, 1861: at 124 Royal. CD, 1866–70: portrait painter, 50 St. Peter St.

Depass, T. M. CD, 1859, 1860: ambrotypist, 110 Poydras.

Diendorf, P. W. CD, 1868: photographic printer at W. H. Leeson's, 167 Poydras.

Dobyns, Thomas Jefferson [T. J.] 1860 Census: born *ca.* 1802 in Tennessee. 1851: vice-president, American Daguerre Association. CD, 1852–59: partner of William H. Harrington, 6 Camp St., N.O. 1853: opened daguerrean gallery in New York City, 303 Broadway, with F. Moissenet and V. L. Richardson; firm won honorable mention at N.Y. world's fair. Dobyns had chain of daguerrean establishments: St. Louis, Memphis, Louisville, Nashville. 1854: disposed of interests in St. Louis, Louisville, Nashville, N.Y.C. galleries. 1856: Dobyns and Harrington employed E. C. Hawkins to make diaphanotypes. 1857: Dobyns and Harrington, 6 Camp St., burned. CD, 1859: living in Amite City, La.
(*DJ*, II [October 15, 1851], 342; *HJ*, V [April 15, 1853], 16; *PAJ*, V [May, 1853], 320; VII [February, 1854], 64; V [January

15, 1854], 299; *HJ*, VI [October 15, 1854], 207; *Bee* March 17, 1856; *Courier*, January 28, 1857)

Downs, —— *ca.* 1866: produced tintypes; developed patented process used by Turner and Cohen.
(Reverse side of a Turner and Cohen tintype of a young boy, in the collection of Margaret Denton Smith)

Dubar, Auguste CD, 1844: daguerreotype portrait maker, c. St. Ann and Bourbon sts.

Dumoulin, F. M. CD, 1870: photographer.

Durand, Prosper E. CD, 1867: photographer, Conti St. near Chartres St.

Dutemple, S. T. CD, 1858: photographer, 90 Bourbon St.

Edwards, Jay Dearborn Born July 14, 1831, in New Hampshire; died June 6, 1900, in Atlanta. 1861: photographic gallery, 19 Royal St., N.O.; war photographer in Pensacola, Fla. 1886: went to Atlanta from Virginia. *Directory of Atlanta, Georgia*, 1886, 1887: gallery of photographic art with Lewis K. Dorman in Atlanta. *Atlanta City Directory*, 1888–1900: Edwards and Son [William M.] photographic gallery in Atlanta.
(Franklin M. Garrett to Mary Louise Tucker, February 27, 1980; *Daily Picayune*, April 9, 1861; May 16, 1861)

Ely, —— [H. G.?] 1844: operator from New York, working in N.O., 3 Exchange Pl.; instructed George S. Cook.
(*Daily Tropic*, January 25, 1844; Account book in Papers of George Smith Cook, Library of Congress)

Emanuel, Simon CD, 1866–68: photographer, 335 Customhouse St.

Enful, Hans 1860 Census: born *ca.* 1833 in Hanover, Germany; 1860: photographer in N.O.

Farrar, Frederick CD, 1870: photographic gallery, 96 Chartres St.

Fleischbein, François 1850 Census: born *ca.* 1804 in Germany. 1833: arrived in N.O.; portrait painter. CD, 1841–57: portrait painter. BD, 1858: associated with photographic gallery, Frenchman St. c. Casacalvo St.
(*L'Abeille*, July 8, 1833)

Foster, W. B CD, 1842: daguerrean, c. Royal and Canal sts. 1842: offered daguerreotype portraits.
(New Orleans *Commercial Bulletin*, March 21, 1842)

Franklin, —— 1847: proprietor, Franklin Daguerreian Rooms, 11 St. Charles St., 71 Canal St.
(*Bee*, January 25, 1847)

Frobus, John H. 1860 Census: born *ca.* 1832 in N.O. CD, 1855, 1856: daguerrean, ambrotypist, 72 Chartres St. 1857: moved to 27 Customhouse St. *ca.* 1859: applied for patent for process of taking pictures on leather. CD, 1861: ambrotypist, 66 Customhouse. 1861: Capt., Beauregard Battn., La. Militia. 1863: operator for William W. Washburn, 113 Canal St.
(*L'Abeille*, January 1, 1857; January 31, 1859; Booth, Vol. II, p. 935; *Bee*, September 24, 1863.)

Gehrke, Ferdinand CD, 1859–61: ambrotypist, 33 Annunciation St.

Girod, Emile 1860 Census: born *ca.* 1831 in France. CD, 1861: ambrotypist, 126 Poydras St.

Giroux, —— 1856: photographer with Hirsch, 142 Canal St.
(*Bee*, March 3, 1856)

Glaze, Joseph CD, 1870: photographer.

Gould, Charles W. CD, 1870: partner of J. A. Sheldon, 151 Canal St.

Graham, Mrs. G. CD, 1868: photographer.

Granier, Joseph CD, 1860, 1861: ambrotypist, 651 Front Levee. 1862: Pvt., 18th La. Infantry; prisoner of war. June, 1865: paroled at Natchitoches.
(Booth, Vol. III, Pt. 1, p. 78)

Gray, T. A. 1858: operator at Dobyns and Harrington, 6 Camp St.
(*PAJ*, XI [August, 1858], 244)

Guay, Edward 1860 Census: born *ca.* 1832 in Canada. CD, 1859: ambrotypist, 126 Poydras St. CD, 1860: at 108 Poydras. CD, 1861: at 112 Canal St. CD, 1867, 1870: photographic artist, 131 Poydras [Lilienthal's address].

Guay, William M. 1860 Census: born *ca.* 1814 in Germany. 1856: with W. E. Mealy in Economic Daguerreotype Gallery; October, alone a 126 Poydras. CD, 1857, BD, 1858, CD, 1859, 1860: at 126 Poydras. CD, 1861: Photographic Temple of Art, 108 Poydras. 1862: 2nd Lt. Col., 1st Div., La. Militia. 1863: new gallery at 75 Camp St. BD, 1865: at 57 Camp. CD, 1867: photographer 71/75 Camp. CD, 1868: photographer, 7 Camp; operator, 157 Poydras. 1868: received awards, best colored photograph on porcelain, best plain photograph on porcelain, Grand Fair, N.O.
(*Courier*, May 11, October 17, 1856; Booth, Vol. VIII, Pt. 1, p. 118; *Daily Picayune*, October 16, 1863; *Report of the Second Annual Grand Fair*)

Gum, J. W. *ca.* 1850s: ambrotypist.
(Baton Rouge *Daily Gazette and Comet*, July 6, 1858.

Gustafson, M. Daguerrean in New York, Baltimore and Cincinnati. 1855: daguerrean, 129 Canal St., N.O. 1856: took over Washburn's old stand.
(*Semi-Weekly Creole*, December 29, 1855; *Courier*, February 7, 1856)

Haering, —— 1860 Census: born *ca.* 1825 in France. BD, 1858: at A. Constant's, 17 Hospital St.

Hall, John Bishop January 20, 1857: patented hallotype. Sold rights to process to Frederick Law in 1858, then to Anderson and Blessing. 1860: in N.O. supervising execution of hallotypes at above firm.
(Root, 312; *PAJ*, XI [August, 1858], 244; *Daily Picayune*, March 25, 1860)

Hamilton, Henry A. CD, 1867: photographer, 495 Dryades St.

Harrington, William H. 1850 Census: born *ca.* 1810 in Pennsylvania; died in N.O. 1830s: faculty member, La Grange College, Alabama. *ca.* 1840: daguerreotype experiments with Frederick A. P. Barnard. October, 1841: daguerreotype business with Barnard in Tuscaloosa, Ala. February, 1842: daguerrean rooms, 93 Canal St., N.O.; May, on Camp St. Fall, 1842: back in Tuscaloosa. 1845: still in Tuscaloosa, painting landscapes. 1847: in N.O., taking care of James Maguire's establishment. CD, 1849, 1850: at 6 Camp St. [Maguire's address]. 1850: partner with James Maguire, 6 Camp St.; purchased patent rights to talbotype process for Louisiana, Alabama, Florida, Georgia, and Texas; advertised hyalotypes. CD, 1852–59: partner with T. J. Dobyns, 6 Camp. 1853: wrote "Hints on Practical Photography" for *HJ*; 1857: firm burned. CD, 1860, 1861: ambrotypist, 6 Camp.
(Saunders, *Early Settlers of Alabama*, 11; *American Journal of Science*, XLI [October, 1841], 352; Chute, *Damn Yankee*, 99–101. *Daily Picayune*, February 8, May 3, 1842; Tuscaloosa *Independent Monitor*, January 8, 1845; Nashville *Daily Union*, August 18, 1847; *Daily Picayune*, March 1, 1850; *Courier*, January 28, 1857.)

Haviland, —— CD, 1851, 1852: daguerrean partner of Heer, 180 Circus St.

Hawkins, Ezekiel C. *ca.* 1843–60, daguerrean in Cincinnati. December, 1845: daguerrean rooms, c. Canal and Exchange Pl., N.O. 1856: employed in firm of Dobyns and Harrington, 6 Camp St., supervised making of diaphanotypes.
(Rinhart, 120; *Daily Picayune*, December 2, 1845; *Bee*, March 16, 1856)

Hedrick, F. S. 1856: daguerrean, ambrotypist, 26 Camp St. December, 1856: partner of John H. Clarke, 94 Canal St. CD, 1857–60: daguerrean, 11 Camp St.
(*Bee*, March 17, 1856; *Daily Orleanian*, December 21, 1856)

Heer, —— CD, 1851, 1852: daguerrean partner of Haviland, 180 Circus St.

Heidingsfelder, Emanuel 1860 Census: born *ca.* 1813 in Bavaria. CD, 1843, 1844: cupper and bleeder in N.O. CD, 1849, 1850: dentist. CD, 1853, 1854: daguerrean, Chartres c. Bienville. CD, 1855, 1856. daguerrean, 190 Barracks St. 1860: jeweler.

Heitzman, A. C. CD, 1866: daguerrean, St. Andrew St. c. Magazine St.

Hinton, M. J. 1861: photographer in Montgomery, Ala. December, 1865: proprietor of Crescent Photographic Gallery, 99 Camp St., N.O. CD, 1866: photographer, 90 Camp. 1866: at Crescent Photographic Gallery, 99 Camp.
(M. J. Hinton to George Smith Cook, April 18, 1861, in Papers of George Smith Cook, Library of Congress; *Daily Picayune*, December 25, 1865; May 1, 1866)

Hinton, R. S. BD, 1865: photographer, 99 Camp St.

Hirsch, —— 1856: partner of Giroux; painted photographs, 142 Canal St. (*Bee*, March 3, 1856)

Honfleur, —— Itinerant artist. 1842: draftsman, teaching drawing in N.O.; daguerrean, briefly, 40 Camp St.
(*Daily Picayune*, March 10, June 18, 1842)

Hord, J. T. CD, 1860: ambrotypist, 135 Poydras. CD, 1861: at 205 Canal.

Hughes, Henry CD, 1867: photographer, 61 Camp St. [Samuel Anderson's address].

Hulbert, John E. 1855–56: daguerrean, 26 Camp St.
(*Daily Picayune*, February 18, 1855; *Daily Crescent*, January 1, 1856)

Hutchings, William Henry 1850 Census: born *ca.* 1807 in Louisiana; died September 15, 1885, in N.O. 1844: pupil of James Maguire in N.O.; November, proprietor, daguerrean establishment, c. Canal and Chartres sts. 1845: partner of H. Whittemore, Orleans Daguerreian Gallery; firm received First Premium for daguerreotypes, at Baton Rouge fair. CD, 1846: at 38 St. Charles. 1847: at 3 Chartres; electromagnetic portraits. CD, 1849–56: Canal c. Chartres. October, 1855–56: at 82 Canal St.
(*Courier*, October 16, 1855, January 1, 1856)

Jackson, —— 1854: daguerrean, 80 Camp St.; moved to 184 Camp.
(*Louisiana State Republican*, July 10, 1854

Jacobs, Edward 1850 Census: born *ca.* 1810 in England. 1844: daguerrean, c. Canal and Camp sts. 1845: partner of C. E. Johnson in Southern

Daguerreotype Portrait Gallery, c. Camp and Canal. 1846: firm received Second Premium, Baton Rouge fair. 1848: operator for White & Co., c. Camp and Canal; made daguerreotype of Zachary Taylor. CD, 1849, 1850: daguerrean at 1 Camp. 1850: at 93 Camp; remained there until 1858. December, 1854: offered talbotype. October, 1855: offered ambrotypes. CD, 1859: firm taken over by L. S. Lipman; Jacobs goes to Europe. 1859: hired at old firm by Lipman. October, 1860: offered ivorytype. 1861: still at 93 Camp; Lipman his assistant. 1863: with George Hay Brown and Walter Ogilvie in National Art Union Photograph Gallery, 93 Camp St. 1864: retired; Gustave Moses and Eugene A. Piffet, successors to E. Jacobs, 93 Camp.
(*Daily Picayune*, July 7, 1844; November 2, 1845; *Gazette*, January 10, 1846, *Commercial Times*, January 20, 1848; *Daily Picayune*, December 24, 1850, December 24, 1854, October 15, 1855, September 18, 1859, October 31, 1860, February 20, 1861, January 30, 1862, November 1, 1863, August 24, 1864)

Jefferson, N. S. CD, 1859–61: ambrotype and photograph gallery, 5 Diamond's Row.

Jockler, Stephen CD, 1870: photographer

Johnson, Charles A. CD, 1868, 1869: proprietor, photographic gallery, 570 Magazine St.

Johnson, Mrs. Charles A. CD, 1869: proprietor, photographic gallery, 572 Magazine St.

Johnson, C. E. [Charles E.?] Possibly Charles E. Johnson, Cleveland daguerrean. 1845: partner of Edward Jacobs in Southern Daguerreotype Portrait Gallery, c. Camp and Canal sts. 1846: firm received Second Premium for daguerreotypes at Baton Rouge fair. 1846: proprietor, Johnson & Co., Camp c. Canal. 1851: partner of Fellows in Cleveland. 1853: left Cleveland for California.
(Welling, 121; *Daily Picayune*, November 2, 1845, March 3, 1846; Baton Rouge *Gazette*, January 10, 1846; *DJ*, II [May 15, 1851], 19; *HJ*, V. [April 15, 1853], 16.

Johnson, D. G. [David G.?] December, 1840: in N.O. experimenting with daguerreotype portraits. David G., portrait painter, engraver in New York 1831–35, 1843–45.
(D. G. Johnson to Samuel F. B. Morse, December 21, 1840, in Papers of Samuel F. B. Morse, Library of Congress; Groce and Wallace, *The New York Historical Society's Dictionary of Artists in America, 1564–1860*, 353.)

Joslyn, J. E. CD, 1869: proprietor, photographic saloon [Joslyn & Paloc].

Kaiser, Joseph *MD*, 1857–58: with T. Lilienthal, Baronne St. c. Poydras St. CD, 1858: photographer, 174 Baronne.

Kammer, Joseph H. CD, 1870: photographer, 884 Magazine St.

Kokernot, James M. CD, 1867: photographic artist, Camp St. c. Commercial St.

Langlumé, P. CD, 1846: daguerrean, 119 Chartres St. 1847: exhibited at Baton Rouge fair.
(Baton Rouge *Gazette*, January 9, 1847)

Langwith, Joseph 1865: with John Weiss, photographic gallery, 75 Camp St. CD, 1867: photographer, Locust St. near Erato St.
(*L'Abeille*, March 8, 1865)

Lansot, A. D. CD, 1841–46: portrait painter. CD, 1846: portrait painter and daguerrean, 33 Toulouse St.

Lavery, J. T. [John T.?] CD, 1861: ambrotypist, 108 Poydras St. 1861: 1st Lt. Capt., 18th La. Infantry. 1862–64: in Confederate army. CD, 1866: ambrotypist, 108 Poydras.
(Booth, Vol. II, Pt. 1, p. 676)

Law, Frederick CD, 1856, 1857, BD, 1858: partner of F. Moissenet, 1 Camp St. CD, 1858–61: photographer, 1 Camp. CD, 1866: ambrotypist.

Leeson, William H. *ca.* 1861: Pvt. Kurcyzn's Co., British Grd., La. Militia. BD, 1865: photographer, 132 Poydras St. CD, 1866: at 167 Poydras. CD, 1867, 1868: partner of H. H. Swymmer, 129 Canal St. CD, 1868, 1869: photographer, 167 Poydras and 129 Canal. CD, 1870: photographer, 129 Canal.
(Booth, Vol. III, Pt. 1, p. 710)

Legras, —— 1865: with A. Persac, photographic gallery, 130 Canal St.; firm bought out by Persac.
(*Bee*, March 27, 1865; *L'Abeille*, May 10, 1865)

Leray, Oscar CD, 1869: photographer, 204 Royal St.

Levering, L. 1860 Census: born *ca.* 1822 in Ireland. 1860: photographer in N.O.

Lilienthal, Julius 1860 Census: born *ca.* 1827 in Frankfurt, Germany. CD, 1856, 1857: jeweler, 126 Poydras St. CD, 1858: F. & J. Lilienthal, daguerreotypes, Baronne St. c. Poydras. CD, 1859: J. Lilienthal, jeweler, 126 Poydras. CD, 1860: at 128 Camp St. 1862: Cannoneer, Washington Artillery, La. BD, 1865: jeweler at 28 Camp St.
(Booth, Vol. III, Pt. 1, p. 760)

Lilienthal, Louis CD, 1867, 1868, 1870: photographer, 131 Poydras St.

Lilienthal, Theodore CD, 1857: daguerrean, 132 Poydras St. MD, 1857–58, with J. Kaiser, Baronne St. c. Poydras. CD, 1858: F. & J. Lilienthal, daguerreotypes, Baronne c. Poydras. 1862: Cannoneer, Washington Artillery, La. 1863: photographer, 102 Poydras. BD, 1865, CD 1866: at 131 Poydras; silver medals, best series of stereoscopic views, best views of public buildings, best views of landscapes; gold medal, best and largest display of photographs, Grand Fair, N.O. CD, 1867: partner of Louis Lilienthal, 131 Poydras; bronze medal, photographic views, Paris Universal Exposition. CD, 1868–70: photographer, 131 Poydras. 1868: honorable mention, best and largest display of photographs; silver medal, best set of photographic views, Grand Fair, N.O. 1869: bronze medal, best set of photographic views, Grand Fair, N.O.
(*L'Abeille*, June 4, 1863; *Reports of the U.S. Commissioners to the Paris Universal Exposition, 1867*; Reports of the Grand Fairs, 1866, 1868, 1869)

Lion, Jules [Lyon] 1850 Census: born *ca.* 1816 in France, died January 10, 1866, in N.O., free man of color. 1831–36: exhibited lithographs at Paris Salon. 1837: opened studio in N.O. March, 1840: exhibited daguerreotype views in N.O.; gave demonstrations. CD, 1842: portrait painter, 106 Royal St. December, 1842: moved to 44 Royal; made painted, lithographic, daguerreotype portraits. 1843: at 44 Royal; experimenting with colored daguerreotypes. November, 1843: opened studio at 3 St. Charles St. lithographic and daguerreotype portraits. CD, 1844: portrait painter, 44 Royal. 1848: with Dominique Canova in art school, 1 Exchange Alley. 1856: executing lithographic portraits. 1865: professor of drawing, Louisiana College, 134 Hospital St.
(Cemetery Records; Paris Salons of 1831, 1833, 1834, 1836; *Le Courrier*, March 10, 1840; *Bee*, December 13, 1842; *L'Abeille*, May 24, November 28, 1843; *Le Courrier*, November 30, 1848; *Daily Picayune*, October 2, 1856; *Bee*, October 12, 1865.)

Lipman, L. S. CD, 1859: successor to Edward Jacobs' photographic establishment, 93 Camp St.; rehires Jacobs. 1860–61: assistant to Jacobs.
(*Daily Picayune*, September 18, 1859; February 20, 1861.)

Lockwood, Dr. James E. 1855: daguerrean, 163 Poydras St. 1856: at 148 Carondelet St. CD, 1858: at 134 Poydras. CD, 1859–61: at 139 Poydras. CD, 1866: still in N.O.
(Louisiana *State Republican*, April 1, 1855: *Daily Picayune*, March 19, 1856)

Lukacsy, G. CD, 1861, 1866: photographer, 294 Chartres.

Maguire, James Born *ca.* 1816 in Belfast, Ireland; died January 1, 1851, in N.O.; pupil of William H. Harrington and F. A. P. Barnard in Tuscaloosa. January, 1842: made daguerreotype portraits in N.O., 31 Canal St. May, 1842: traveled to Natchez, Vicksburg, Plaquemine; June, in Baton Rouge taking daguerreotype portraits. 1843, 1844: First Premiums, Baton Rouge fair. 1844: moved to 8 Camp St. 1845: Second Premium, Baton Rouge fair; August, at 1 Camp, c. Canal. CD, 1846: daguerrean, 6 Camp St.; First Premium for daguerreotypes, Baton Rouge fair. 1847: visiting daguerrean in Nashville. 1848: First Premium, Baton Rouge fair. 1850: partner with William Harrington, 6 Camp St.; purchased rights to talbotype for Louisiana, Alabama, Florida, Georgia, Texas; advertised the hyalotype.
(*Daily Picayune*, January 2, 1851, April 6, 1842, January 28, 1842, May 20, 1842; Baton Rouge *Gazette*, June 11 and 18, 1842; January 21, 1843; *Daily Picayune*, January 14, 1844; *Courier*, May 29, 1844; Baton Rouge *Gazette*, May 17, 1845; *Daily Picayune*, August 25, 1845; Baton Rouge *Gazette*, January 10, 1846; Nashville *Daily Union*, August 18, 1847; *Daily Picayune*, March 1, 1850)

Malone, William BD, 1865: photographer, 523 Tchoupitoulas St.

Mancell, Henry CD, 1868: photographer. CD, 1869: photographic saloon, 75 Camp St.

Marmer, Caliste [Charles Marmu?] CD, 1867: photographic artist, 133 Esplanade St.

Marmont, Joseph CD, 1870: photographer,

Marmu, Charles 1860 Census: born *ca.* 1820 in France, probably the Marma who was photographic partner of Picard, 106 Royal St., in 1854; previously an operator in Paris. *MD*, 1857–58: daguerrean, 117 Royal. CD, 1858–60: at 117 Royal. CD, 1861: at Royal c. Conti St. 1863: photographic gallery, 69 Royal. BD, 1865: at 60 Royal. CD, 1867: photographic artist, 133 Esplanade St. CD, 1868–70: photographer, 111 Royal.
(*Courier*, December 20, 1854; *L'Abeille*, May 8, 1863)

Mary, Victor CD, 1866: photographer with Bonnemer, 96 Chartres St. CD, 1869: photographer, 233 Orleans St.

McPherson, William D. Born *ca.* 1833 in Boston, Mass.; died October 9, 1867, in N.O. CD, 1856, 1860–61: ambrotypist, photographer in Concord, N.H. 1862: ambrotypist, photographer in Baton Rouge. 1863: working in Baton Rouge with Oliver; *cartes-de-visite* views of the city. BD, 1865: McPherson and Oliver in N.O., 133 Canal St. CD, 1866, 1867: photographer, 132 Canal; in 1867, offered opaltype.

(Succ. Records; Baton Rouge *Weekly Gazette and Comet*, December 31, 1862; *Daily Picayune*, January 15, 1867)

Mealy, W. E. 1856: with William Guay in Economic Daguerreotype Gallery, 126 Poydras St. *MD*, 1857–58: Mealy & Co., ambrotypists, 128 Poydras. CD, 1858: partner in Mealy & Co. with Charles Parker, 128 Poydras. CD, 1859–61: at 128 Poydras. CD, 1866, ambrotypist, 181½ Poydras.
(*Courier*, May 11, 1856)

Miller, H. 1866: dealer in photographs, 69 Canal St.

Milter, Henry CD, 1867: photographer, 7 St. Charles St.

Moissenet, F. [Felix] 1850 Census: born *ca.* 1814 in France. CD, 1849, 1850: daguerrean, 134 Royal St. March, 1850: at 28 Camp St. CD, 1852–55: at c. Camp and Canal sts. 1853: opened daguerrean establishment with Dobyns and Richardson in New York City; received honorable mention for daguerreotypes, New York world's fair. CD, 1856, 1857, BD, 1858: partner of Frederick Law, 1 Camp. December, 1858: opened new photographic gallery, 6 Camp. CD, 1859: with W. W. Washburn & Co., 142 Canal. CD, 1860, 1861: ambrotypist, 6 Camp.
(*Daily Picayune*, March 5, 1850; *Bee*, March 13, 1850; *HJ*, V [April 15, 1853], 16; V [January 15, 1854], 299; *PAJ*, VII [February, 1854], 64; *L'Abeille*, December 23, 1858)

Moore, Justus E. 1841: made daguerreotypes of Andrew Jackson at the Hermitage. 1842: briefly daguerrean in N.O., c. Baronne and Canal sts.
(New Orleans *Commercial Bulletin*, March 25, 1842)

Moses, Bernard Born November 22, 1832, in Bavaria; died September 24, 1899, in N.O.; son of Samuel Moses. 1850, Census: jeweler in N.O. *MD*, 1857–58, CD, 1857–61: partner in ambrotype, photographic gallery with brother Gustave Moses [B. & G. Moses], 46 Camp St. 1861: Capt., 21st (Kennedy's) La. Infantry. 1864: mustered out of service. CD, 1866: ambrotypist, 1 Camp. CD, 1867–69 with B. & G. Moses, 1 Camp. CD, 1870: at 92 Canal/1 Camp.
(*Daily Picayune*, September 25, 1899; Booth, Vol. III, Pt. 1, p. 1071)

Moses, Edward R. 1860 Census: born *ca.* 1833 in Bavaria; died January 16, 1905; son of Samuel Moses. CD, 1857: daguerrean, Camp St. c. Poydras St. *ca.* 1861: 2nd Lt., 1st Div., La. Militia. CD, 1867, 1868: in business with father [S. Moses & Son], 26 Camp. CD, 1869: at 46 Camp. CD, 1870: at 165 Canal St.
(*Daily Picayune*, January 17, 1905; Booth, Vol. III, Pt. 1, p. 1071)

Moses, Gustave A. 1860 Census: born *ca.* 1836 in Bavaria; died October 23, 1915,

in N.O.; son of Samuel Moses. 1854: opened daguerrean saloon, offered stereoscopic portraits, 54 Camp St. CD, 1855: at 54 Camp. *MD*, 1857–58, CD, 1857–61: partner of Bernard Moses [B. & G. Moses], 46 Camp. 1861: 1st Lt., 21st (Kennedy's) La. Infantry. 1864: with E. A. Piffet, successor to Jacobs, 93 Camp. CD, 1867–69: with B. & G. Moses, 1 Camp. CD, 1870: at 92 Canal/1 Camp.
(*Times Picayune*, October 24, 1915; *Daily Orleanian*, December 23, 1854; Booth, Vol. III, Pt. 1, p. 1071; *Daily Picayune*, August 26, 1864)

Moses, Louis Son of Samuel Moses. *MD*, 1857–58, CD, 1857, CD 1858: photographer, ambrotype saloon, 26 Camp St. 1862: Pvt., 4th Regt. European Brig. La. Militia. CD, 1866: partner of A. Constant, 21 Hospital St. CD, 1867: A Constant & Moses, 30/21 Hospital St.
(Warren G. Moses to LSM, March 19, 1979; Booth, Vol. III, Pt. 1, p. 1071)

Moses, Nicolas 1860 Census: born *ca.* 1803 in Germany. 1860: ambrotypist in N.O.

Moses, Samuel Wolfgang Born December 17, 1798, in Bavaria; died July 12, 1885, in N.O. Father of Bernard, Edward R., Gustave A., and Louis. *ca.* 1830s: came to N.O.; trained as a chemist. CD, 1850: daguerrean, 230 Royal St. CD, 1851–61: daguerrean, c. Camp and Poydras sts. 1861: Pvt. 11th La. Infantry. BD, 1865, CD, 1866: Moses & Son, Camp c. Gravier St. CD, 1867: S. Moses & Son, 26 Camp. CD, 1868: listing at 49 Camp; advertisement, at 46 Camp. CD, 1869: photographic saloon, 40 Camp. CD, 1870: S. Moses & Son, 165 Canal St.
(Cemetery Records; Warren G. Moses to LSM, March 19, 1979; Booth, Vol. III, Pt. 1, p. 1072)

Nanitz, L. D. CD, 1870: photographer.

Neuland, J. W. 1845: daguerrean, 124 Royal St.
(*Daily Tropic*, May 24, 1845)

Newton, E. H., Jr. CD, 1860: proprietor, scenic and photographic gallery, 19 Royal St.

Noessel, G. CD, 1846: daguerrean, 18 Royal St. 1847: at c. Poydras and Camp sts.; December, in Vera Cruz making daguerreotypes.
(*Daily Delta*, April 25, 1847; *Daily Picayune*, January 1, 1848)

Nonenmacher, H. CD, 1868: photographer, 294 St. Ann St.

Nystrand, Charles CD, 1843, 1844: "daguerreotype drawer," 165 Chartres St. CD, 1846: apothecary.

Oden, W. H. CD, 1856: daguerrean.

Ogilvie, Walter 1863: partner of Edward Jacobs and George Hay Brown in National Art Union Photograph Gallery, 93 Camp St. (*Daily Picayune*, November 1, 1863)

Oliver, —— 1863: working in Baton Rouge with W. D. McPherson; *cartes-de-visite* views of the city. BD, 1865: with McPherson, 133 Canal St.

Olsen, N. [U?] 1860 Census: born *ca.* 1830 in Denmark. CD, 1861: photographer, 121 Chartres St. 1862: *N.* Olsen, Pvt., Chalmette Regt., La. Militia. BD, 1865: at 122 Poydras St. CD, 1866: *U.* Olsen, photographer, 157 Poydras. CD, 1867: *N.* Olsen, at 157 Poydras. (Booth, Vol. III, Pt. 2, p. 30)

Orthman, Henry CD, 1868: photographer.

Osborne, John 1860 Census: born *ca.* 1810 in Maine. 1860: daguerrean in N.O.

Palmer, Archibald L. Born *ca.* 1838 in Kentucky; 1861: Pvt. 6th La. Infantry; 1862: deserted; occupation: painter. CD, 1867: photographic operator, 57 Camp St. [Turner & Cohen's address]. CD, 1868: operator at 61 Camp St. [S. Anderson's address]. CD, 1869: photographic saloon, 167 Poydras. CD, 1870: photographer. (Booth, Vol. III, Pt. 2, pp. 61–62)

Palmer, J. R. Before 1846: daguerrean in N.O., 56 Canal St. [address of Plumbe's gallery in 1844]; 1845: photographer in Galveston, Texas; 1846: photographer in Corpus Christi, Tex. (Galveston *Gazette*, December 15, 1845; Corpus Christi *Gazette*, January 8, 1846)

Paloc, Lewis [Palloc] CD, 1869: proprietor, photographic saloon [Joslyn & Paloc]. CD, 1870: photographer, 280 Common St.

Parker, Charles W. CD, 1858–61: partner of W. E. Mealy [Mealy & Co.], 128 Poydras.

Paul, Peter CD, 1868: photographic operator, 131 Poydras St. [Lilienthal's address]. CD, 1870: photographer, 489 Annunciation St.

Persac, A. [Adrien?] Probably the painter and architect Adrien Persac who was born in 1823 and died in 1873. 1856: photographic partner of William G. Vail, Baton Rouge. 1865: partner of Legras, photographic gallery, 130 Canal St.; later bought out Legras. CD, 1867, 1868: architect, 83 Exchange Pl. 1869: at Academy of Drawing, 75 Camp St. (*Daily Advocate*, July 15, 1856; *Bee*, March 27, 1865; *L'Abeille*, May 10, 1865; *Bee*, January 26, 1869)

Petty, J. W. 1860 Census: born *ca.* 1834 in Missouri. *MD*, 1857–58, CD, 1859: proprietor, ambrotype, photograph gallery, 136 Poydras St. CD, 1860, 1861: at 132 Poydras. BD, 1865: photographer, 106 Poydras. CD, 1866: at 135 Poydras. CD, 1867: at 135 and 181½ Poydras. CD, 1868: at 161 Poydras. CD, 1869, photographic gallery, 161½ Poydras. CD, 1870: at 161/161½ Poydras.

Pey, Thomas [Pye?] CD, 1870: photographer.

Peyroux, Charles CD, 1846: daguerrean, c. Royal and St. Peter sts.

Phillips, L. A. CD, 1852, 1853: daguerrean, 28 Camp St.

Picard, —— 1854: photographic partner of Marma [Marmu], 106 Royal St. (*Courier*, December 20, 1854)

Piffet, Eugene A. August, 1864: with Gustave Moses, successor to Edward Jacobs' gallery, 93 Camp St. CD, 1866: proprietor, photographic and fine art gallery [National Gallery of Art], 93 Camp; manufacturing albumenized paper.
(*Daily Picayune*, August 26, 1864; *Bee*, July 29, 1865; New Orleans *Times*, August 7, 1865)

Plumbe, John, Jr. Born 1809 in Wales. 1841–50: chain of daguerreotype galleries in America. 1844: opened branch gallery in N.O., 56 Canal St. (Newhall, 151; *Daily Picayune*, November 21, 1844)

Pointel Du Portail, J. B. Born in France; pupil of Jacques-Louis David and others; portrait and miniature painter, lithographer. 1836: teacher of painting and drawing in N.O. 1837: lithographic artist for *Bee*. February, 1840: advertised exhibition of daguerreotype views of New Orleans: May, advertised intended exhibition in Baton Rouge. 1844: living in Baton Rouge; received award for painted portraits, Baton Rouge fair.
(*L'Abeille*, November 9, 1836; *Bee*, April 5, 1837; *L'Abeille*, February 11, 1840; Baton Rouge *Gazette*, May 2, 1840; *Daily Picayune*, January 14, 1844.)

Pollock, Lewis CD, 1868: photogapher, 280 Common St.

Prince, Louis Isaac Born *ca.* 1832 in Ireland; died October 22, 1867 in N.O. *ca.* 1861: Pvt., 2nd La. Cav.; roll of prisoners of war, CSA. 1865: paroled. BD, 1865, CD, 1866: photographer, 112 Canal St. CD, 1867: at 112 Canal; then moved to 8 St. Charles St. CD, 1868: at 8 St. Charles.
(Succ. Records; Booth, Vol. III, Pt. 2, p. 206)

Ranney, —— 1854: daguerrean, 80 Camp St.
(*Daily Picayune*, February 12, 1854)

Roberts, C. F. 1860 Census: Born *ca.* 1832 in Germany. 1860: daguerrean in N.O.

Roberts, John CD, 1867: black photographer, 181½ Poydras [J. W. Petty's address]. CD, 1870: photographer, 281 Gravier St.

Robira, Louis CD, 1868: photographic operator at S. Anderson's, 61 Camp St. CD, 1870: photographer, 202 Royal St.; then 200 Royal. (*L'Abeille*, June 11, 1869)

Rodgers, Stephen CD, 1867: photographer, 214 Canal.

Roesberg, George F. CD, 1870: photographer in N.O.

Root, Marcus A. Born 1808 in Granville, Ohio; died 1888 in Philadelphia; had several daguerreotype galleries in America. *ca.* 1844–45: daguerrean in N.O. (Rinharts, 127; Root, 365)

Rosenberger, G. L. BD, 1865: photographer, 270 Magazine St. CD, 1866, 1867: proprietor, photograph gallery, 568 Magazine.

Roth, Andrew BD, 1865: photographer, 368 Old Levee St. CD, 1866, 1867: at 368 Victory St. CD, 1869: artist, painter, photographer, 368 Victory. CD, 1870: portrait painter and photographer, 368 Decatur St.

Rudd, A. G. CD, 1870: photographer in N.O.

Sancan, Victor CD, 1854: daguerrean, 80 Camp St.

Schleier, Theodore M. [Shleier] 1857: at daguerreotype saloon, Chartres St. *MD*, 1857–58, CD, 1859, 1860: at 184 Camp St. *Nashville City and Business Directory*, 1860–61: photographic operator at C. C. Gier's, Nashville, Tenn. 1866: had photographic gallery in Nashville. (*Courier*, February 13, 1857; *HJ*, XVIII [August 15, 1866], 123.)

Scoggins, James H. CD, 1861: ambrotypist, 538 Magazine St. CD, 1870: at 185 Poydras.

Scoggins, Thomas R. 1861: Pvt. 22nd and 23rd La. Infantry; November, discharged. CD, 1868: photographic saloon, 181½ Poydras. (Booth, Vol. III, Pt. 2, p. 490)

Seligman, Mrs. C. CD, 1870: photographer, 181½ Poydras.

Seligman, Samuel CD, 1869, 1870: photographer, 181½ Poydras.

Sheldon, James A. 1864, BD, 1865, CD, 1866–68: photographic gallery 101 Canal St. CD, 1870: partner of C. W. Gould, 151 Canal St. (*Daily Picayune*, December 1, 1864)

Simon, Eugene CD, 1870: operator at A. Constant's, 21 Hospital St.

Souby, Edward J. CD, 1870: photographer, 572 Magazine St.

Souley, E. J. CD, 1870: photographer, 568 Magazine St.

Souliar, P. CD, 1859–61: daguerrean, Baronne St. c. Poydras St.

Spieler, George J. 1860 Census: born *ca.* 1840 in Pennsylvania. 1860: photographer in N.O.

Spillman, Henry BD, 1865, CD, 1867: photographer, 91 Spain St.

Stach, Francis L. CD, 1870: photographer.

Swymmer, H. H. BD, 1865: photographer, 147 Canal St. CD, 1867, 1868: had photographic gallery with Leeson, 129 Canal St.

Treihl, W. V. 1860 Census: born *ca.* 1824 in Poland. 1860: photographer in N.O.

Turner, Austin Augustus Born in North Carolina; died September 29, 1866 in N.O. *Trow's New York City Directory*, 1855–56: photographer in New York City, 349 Broadway St. *Boston City Directory*, 1856, 1857, 1858, 1860: partner with J. A. Cutting, 10 Tremont Row, Boston. *Trow's New York City Directory*, 1860–61, 1861–62: in N.Y.C., lithographer, 553 Broadway. *Trow's New York City Directory*, 1862–63, 1863–64: photographer in N.Y.C., 15 Mercer St. *Trow's New York City Directory*, 1864–65, 1865–66: firm at 765 Broadway. With Dr. Wm. Dutton, photographic assistant, took views of fortifications in Washington, D.C., soon after first Battle of Bull Run. 1864: associated with Samuel Anderson in N.O., 61 Camp St. March, 1865: proprietor of New Orleans Photographic Company, 57 Camp St. July, 1866: partner of Warren A. Cohen [Turner & Cohen], 57 Camp St.; prize for best photograph in watercolors, Grand Fair, N.O.; sold tintypes made by Downs' patent process.
(Orleans Parish Death Records, NOPL; Succ. Records; *PAJ*, III [October, 1856], 320; *Daily Picayune*, November 8, November 19, 1864: February 26, July 29, 1865; July 7, 1866; *Report of the First Annual Grand Fair*)

Washburn, Alonzo L. CD, 1869: photographer, 113 Canal St. CD, 1870: assistant operator at W. W. Washburn's, 113 Canal.

Washburn, Charles H. CD, 1869: photographer, 113 Canal St. CD, 1870: clerk, W. W. Washburn's, 113 Canal.

Washburn, Lorenzo S. Born *ca.* 1822 in New Hampshire; died April 7, 1907; brother of William W. Washburn: partners with William in photographic business, beginning in 1850. CD, 1867–70: photographer, 113 Canal St.
(*Daily Picayune*, November 16, 1903; April 8, 1907)

Washburn, William Watson 1860 Census: born *ca.* 1827 in Peterboro, N.H.; died November 15, 1903, in N.O. *New York Mercantile Register*, 1849–50:

daguerrean in New York City, 252 Broadway St. November, 1849: opened New York Daguerrean Establishment in N.O., 29 Camp St. 1850, CD, 1852, 1853: at 26 Camp St., November, 1853: moved to 120 Canal [Touro's Building]. CD, 1854–57: at 120 Canal St. CD, 1858–60: at 142 Canal. CD, 1861, BD, 1865, CD, 1870: photographer, 113 Canal St. 1866, 1868: prizes for best plain photograph, best photograph on porcelain, Grand Fairs, N.O.
(Orleans Parish Death Records, NOPL; *Daily Picayune*, November 16, 1903; November 15, 1849; December 21, 1850; November 25, 1853: Reports on the Grand Fairs, 1866, 1868.)

Weiss, John 1865: with Joseph Langwith, photographic gallery, 75 Camp St. (*L'Abeille*, March 8, 1865)

White, Edward *Doggett's New York City Directory*, 1842–1846: jewel case maker, then daguerrean and manufacturer of photographic materials in New York City. 1846: had E. White & Co., daguerreotype gallery and furnishing establishment in N.O., c. Camp and Canal sts.; took over Johnson's Southern Daguerreotype Portrait Gallery. 1848: employed Edward Jacobs.
(*Daily Picauyne*, October 6, 1846; *L'Abeille*, October 8, 1846; *Bee*, March 8, 1847; *Commercial Times*, January 20, 1848)

Whittemore, H. 1845: partner of William Hutchings in Orleans Daguerreian Gallery; First Premium for daguerreotypes, Baton Rouge fair. 1846: daguerrean, 10 Camp St. 1848: at 10 Camp, then at 15 Camp. 1851: exhibited daguerreotype views of New Orleans, Fair of the American Institute, New York City.
(*Daily Picayune*, July 3, 1845; December 20, 1846; *Southern Traveller*, January 5, 1848; *Daily Picayune*, January 23, 1848; *DJ*, II [October 15, 1851], 341.)

Wiley, J. H. CD, 1869: photographic gallery, c. Magazine & St. Andrew sts.

Notes

Introduction

1 *L'Abeille de la Nouvelle-Orléans*, March 14, 1840.
2 *Ibid.*, November 29, 1841.
3 William Welling, *Photography in America: The Formative Years, 1839–1900* (New York, 1978), 14.
4 *Ibid.*, 199.
5 *Ibid.*, 211.

I

1 Roger W. Shugg, *Origins of Class Struggle in Louisiana: A Social History of White Farmers and Laborers During Slavery and After, 1840–1875* (Baton Rouge, 1939), 2.
2 New Orleans *Commercial Bulletin*, December 9, 1839.
3 A. Oakey Hall, *The Manhattaner in New Orleans: Or, Phases of Crescent City Life* (Baton Rouge, 1976), 32–33, originally published in 1851; R. G. Barnwell (ed.), *The New-Orleans Book* (New Orleans, 1851), x.
4 Shugg, *Origins of Class Struggle*, 53–54.
5 Robert C. Reinders, *End of an Era: New Orleans, 1850–1860* (New Orleans, 1964), 54.
6 William Dunlap, *Diary of William Dunlap* (New York, 1830), III, 785.
7 New Orleans *Daily Picayune*, January 2, August 17, 1841.
8 Full accounts of the early history of photography may be found in Beaumont Newhall, *The History of Photography* (4th ed., New York, 1964), and Helmut Gernsheim and Alison Gernsheim, *The History of Photography: From the Camera Obscura to the Beginning of the Modern Era* (New York, 1969). The classic history of photography in America is found in Robert Taft, *Photography and the American Scene: A Social History, 1839–1889* (Dover, 1964), originally published in 1938. Also see Welling, *Photography in America*, for a recent updated history.
9 Gernsheim and Gernsheim, *The History of Photography*, 120.
10 "Photogenic Drawing," *United States Magazine and Democratic Review*, V (May, 1839), 517–20.
11 New Orleans *Bee*, October 24, 1839.
12 Beaumont Newhall, *The Daguerreotype in America* (3rd rev. ed.; New York, 1976), 28.
13 *Bee*, January 22, 1840. The Gernsheims state, in *L. J. M. Daguerre: The History of the Diorama and the Daguerreotype* (Rev. ed.; New York, 1956), 135, that Gouraud did exhibit in New Orleans, "where his daguerreotype collection was destroyed by fire in January 1843." However, *Niles' Weekly Register*, February 11, 1843, and the *Bee*, January 5 and 31, 1843, describe four imported dioramas, not daguerreotypes, and their destruction by fire.
14 Letter, in Papers of Samuel F. B. Morse, Manuscript Division, Library of Congress.
15 *Bee*, March 14, 1840.
16 *Ibid.*
17 H. W. Janson (comp.), *Catalogues of the Paris Salon, 1673 to 1881* (New York,

1977). For another version of Lion's origins, see Regina A. Perry, *Selections of 19th Century Afro-American Art* (New York, 1976).

18 *Gazette de Baton Rouge*, August 12, 1837.

19 G. D. Coulon to B. A. Wikstrom, March 24, 1901, in Scrapbook "Artists of New Orleans and Their Pictures," Louisiana State Museum Library.

20 *Bee*, April 9, 1840; Baton Rouge *Gazette*, May 2, 1840.

21 Baton Rouge *Gazette*, April 18, 1840.

22 *Bee*, March 28, 1840.

23 Welling, *Photography in America*, 7–22.

24 D. G. Johnson to Samuel F. B. Morse, December 31, 1840, in Morse Papers.

25 *L'Abeille de la Nouvelle-Orléans*, November 27, 1841.

26 *Bee*, April 30, 1841.

27 *Ibid.*, September 8, 1841, quoting the Washington, D.C., *National Intelligencer*

II

1 *Pitts & Clarke's Guide and Directory, New Orleans, Lafayette, Algiers, & Gretna*, 1842. *Commercial Bulletin*, January 26, 1842.

2 *Commercial Bulletin*, March 21, March 29, 1842.

3 *Daily Picayune*, January 28, 1842.

4 *Ibid.*, May 20, 1842; Baton Rouge *Gazette*, June 11, 1842; James Edmonds Saunders, *Early Settlers of Alabama* (New Orleans, 1899), Pt. 1, p. 11; F. A. P. Barnard to Samuel F. B. Morse, May 19, 1841, in Morse Papers; F. A. P. Barnard, "Improvement in the Daguerreotype Process of Photography," *American Journal of Science and Arts*, XLI (October, 1841), 352–54.

5 William Joseph Chute, *Damn Yankee! The First Career of Frederick A. P. Barnard, Educator, Scientist, Idealist* (Port Washington, N.Y., 1978), 99.

6 *Daily Picayune* and *L'Abeille de la Nouvelle-Orléans*, February 8, 1842; *Daily Picayune*, May 3, 1842; Chute, *Damn Yankee*, 101.

7 *Commercial Bulletin*, March 25, 1842. See Welling, *Photography in America*, 48–49, for a discussion of the several men who photographed Jackson in 1845.

8 *Daily Picayune*, June 18, April 22, 1842.

9 *Bee*, December 12, 1842; *L'Abeille de la Nouvelle-Orléans*, January 6, 1843.

10 Particularly in the 1840s the mourning portrait became a popular memorial to deceased loved ones and several artists were advertising their services for this purpose. See *Louisiana Courier*, November 24, 1840.

11 Abraham Bogardus, "The Lost Art of the Daguerreotype," *Century Magazine*, LXVIII (May, 1904), 91.

12 Richard Rudisill, *Mirror Image: The Influence of the Daguerreotype on American Society* (Albuquerque, 1971), 205, quoting *Godey's Lady's Book*, XXXVIII (May, 1849), 355.

13 Eliza Ripley, *Social Life in Old New Orleans: Being Recollections of My Girlhood* (New York, 1912), 125; *Ballou's Dollar Monthly Magazine*, II (December, 1855), 593; *Daguerreian Journal*, I (January 15, 1851), 144.

14 Clara Solomon Diary, in Department of Archives and Manuscripts, Troy H. Middleton Library, Louisiana State University.

15 George Smith Cook Notebook, in Papers of George Smith Cook, Manuscript Division, Library of Congress.

16 *Commercial Bulletin*, March 25, 1842.

17 *Bee*, May 24, 1843. *Le Courrier de la Louisiane*, March 18, 1843; Baton Rouge *Gazette*, April 1, 1843. Maguire's notice in the *Daily Picayune* of January 5, 1843, did not mention color. Two lawsuits against Jules Lion in 1844 may have had something to do with the disappearance of his newspaper advertisements from 1844 to 1848. *Le Courrier de la Louisiane*, March 5, October 28, 1844.

18 *Commercial Bulletin*, January 24, 1844. Floyd Rinhart and Marion Rinhart, *American Daguerreian Art* (New York, 1967), 124, speak of Mayr as a daguerreotypist.

19 Marcus A. Root, *The Camera and the Pencil, or the Heliograhpic Art* (Philadelphia, 1864), 365; A. D. Cohen, "George S. Cook and the Daguerrean Art," *Photographic Art-Journal*, I (May, 1851), 285. Ely later published a New York magazine called the *Ladies' Wreath*. George Cooke (1793–1849) was a portrait, historical, and landscape painter who was born in Maryland. He was in New Orleans from about 1844 to 1847, then again in 1849. George C. Groce and David H. Wallace, *The New-York Historical Society's Dictionary of Artists in America, 1564–1860* (New Haven, 1957), 145–46.

20 *Daily Picayune*, July 7, 1844. Several sources on photography, including the Rinharts' *American Daguerreian Art*, have referred to an *Emil* Jacobs, "Portrait painter, art dealer, and daguerrean" working at 73 Camp Street around 1850. *Edward* Jacobs, who had a gallery at *93* Camp Street during the 1850s, was the same Jacobs who came to the city in the 1840s, as several advertisements testify. *Bee*, October 17, 1855; *Daily Picayune*, November 4, 1863.

21 Baton Rouge *Gazette*, January 21, 1843, January 13, 1844. At the 1844 fair, J. B. Pointel du Portail received a certificate for painted portraits. *Daily Picayune*, January 14, 1844. These fairs continued through the next two decades.

22 *Louisiana Courier*, May 29, 1844.

23 *Daily Picayune*, July 10, 1844.

24 *Louisiana Courier*, June 1, 1844.

25 Baton Rouge *Gazette*, May 17, 1845.

26 New Orleans *Daily Tropic*, June 4–20, 1845.

27 Reese V. Jenkins, *Images and Enterprise* (Baltimore, 1975), 16, is a thorough study of photographic technology and the American photographic industry from 1839 to 1925.

28 *New Orleans As It Is, by a Resident* (New Orleans [?], 1850), 31–32.

29 *Daily Picayune*, December 20, 1846; New Orleans *Commercial Times*, April 9, 1847; *Daguerreian Journal*, II (October 15, 1851), 342. See Newhall, *Daguerreotype in America*, 120.

30 Baton Rouge *Gazette*, January 10, 1846.

31 According to the *Daguerreian Journal*, II (May 15, 1851), 19, C. E. Johnson was at that time practicing daguerreotyping with Mr. P. Fellows in Cleveland. *Daily Picayune*, October 6, 1846.

32 *Commercial Times*, January 20, 1848. A portrait of Taylor in the collection of the Chicago Historical Society can be attributed to Jacobs by notes inscribed on the verso. Jules Lion and Jacques Amans also made portraits of Taylor at this time.

33 *L'Abeille de la Nouvelle-Orléans*, January 14, 1848; Martha E. Battle to Mary Louise Tucker, August 15, 1979.

34 *Daily Picayune*, November 21, 1844. Plumbe had galleries in fourteen other cities. Taft, *Photography and the American Scene*, 51.

35 *Daily Picayune*, November 15, 1849; November 16, 1903.

36 Nashville *Daily Union*, August 18, 1847.

37 James Herring and J. B. Longacre (eds.), *National Portrait Gallery of Distinguished Americans, with Biographical Sketches* (Philadelphia, 1854), II.

38 *Daily Picayune*, May 30, 1849.

39 *New Orleans Pictorial Advertiser*, 1849.

40 *Ibid.*

III

1 Shugg, *Origins of Class Struggle*, 109.

2 Leon Cyprian Soulé, *The Know-Nothing Party in New Orleans: A Reappraisal* (Baton Rouge, 1961), 61; Reinders, *End of an Era*, 42.

3 Taft, *Photography and the American Scene*, 69.

4 For further information on these journals, see Newhall, *Daguerreotype in America*, 169, 34–35.

5 For an indication that New Orleans photographers subscribed to the national journals, see *Humphrey's Journal*, VI (April 15, 1854), 9.

6 *Daguerreian Journal*, II (October 15, 1851), 342–43.

7 *New Orleans City Directory*, 1851; *Affleck's Southern Rural Almanac*, (1851), 121.

8 *Daily Picayune*, March 1, 1850; New Orleans *Daily Crescent*, March 1, 1850; *Louisiana Spectator*, April 12, 1850.

9 *Photographic Art-Journal*, II (August, 1851), 99; Index of Successions, Fourth District Court, Orleans Parish 1437, filed January 6, 1851, in New Orleans Public Library.

10 *Daguerreian Journal*, I (November 15, 1850), 64.

11 *Photographic Art-Journal*, V (May, 1853), 320; *Humphrey's Journal*, V (January 15, 1854), 299. The same journal noted of the peripatetic New Orleans photographer, "Dobyns, of almost everywhere, is doing well" (p. 302). *Ibid.*, V (April 15, 1853), 16, had announced that Dobyns and Richardson were about to open a gallery with [Moissenet].

12 *Humphrey's Journal*, V (April 15, 1853), 12–15.

13 *Ibid.* (May 15, 1853), 44–48.

14 Welling, *Photography in America*, 103, discusses the stereoscope. Barnard's article appeared in *American Journal of Science and Arts*, XVI (November, 1853) 348–50. On J. G. Barnard, see Chute, *Damn Yankee*, 6.

15 *Daily Orleanian*, December 23, 1854; *Daily Picayune*, December 13, 1859.

16 *Humphrey's Journal*, V (February 15, 1854), 335, VI (October 15, 1854), 207.

17 *Daily Picayune*, January 2, 1851. Invitations addressed to the ladies occur throughout the period. The advertiser was informing the ladies that his establishment was suitable for their genteel natures. To accommodate their vanities, one firm even provided the ladies with a hairdresser at the studio, free of charge. *L'Abeille de la Nouvelle-Orléans*, April 1, 1865.

18 *Louisiana Courier*, December 6, 1853; *Humphrey's Journal*, V (August 1, 1853), 127, V (January 1, 1854), 287.

19 *Humphrey's Journal*, VI (May 1, 1854), 31.

20 *Louisiana Courier*, July 26, 1855.

21 *Daily Picayune*, March 5, 1850.

22 Warren G. Moses to Louisiana State Museum, March 19, 1979.

23 *Daily Picayune*, November 15, 1849.

24 *Daily Picayune*, November 16, 1903, November 25, 1853.

25 *Humphrey's Journal*, VI (July 1, 1854), 81.

26 Welling, *Photography in America*, 107, 197–98. The Cutting patent was to cause controversy in the 1860s.

27 Taft, *Photography and the American Scene*, 122; *Humphrey's Journal*, VI (September 15, 1854), 169.

28 *Daily Picayune*, January 11, 1855; Welling, *Photography in America*, 95.

29 *Bee*, October 17, 1855; *Daily Picayune*, October 15, 1855.

30 Samuel C. Busey, "Early History of Daguerreotypy in the City of Washington," *Records of the Columbia Historical Society*, III (1900), 93; Root, *The Camera and the Pencil*, 366.

31 Busey, "Early History of Daguerreotypy," 93.

32 *Daily Picayune*, February 10, 1856; *Daily Orleanian*, December 21, 1856.

33 R. A. Carnden, "New Orleans Photographic Galleries," *Photographic and Fine-Art Journal*, XI (August, 1858), 244–45.

34 *Daily Picayune*, December 2, 1856.

35 Taft, *Photography and the American Scene*, 130; Nathan G. Burgess, *The Photograph Manual: A Practical Treatise . . .* (New York: 1973), 69–70.

36 *New Orleans Merchants' Diary and Guide*, I (1857), 40.

37 *Bee*, March 16–17, 1856. See Welling, *Photography in America*, 59, for discussion of early collodion experiments, and Root, *The Camera and the Pencil*, 309, for a description of the diaphanotype.

38 *Bee*, March 17, 1856; *Louisiana Courier*, January 28, 1857.

39 Carnden, "New Orleans Photographic Galleries," 244.

40 Records of Conveyances, in Tangipahoa Parish [formerly part of Saint Helena Parish] Courthouse. He owned at his death about 550 acres in the parish. According to Saunders, *Early Settlers of Alabama*, 11, Harrington died in New Orleans.

41 *Gardner's New Orleans Directory* 1859–1861.

42 *Daily Picayune*, November 1, 1856: *Louisiana Courier*, October 24, 1856.
43 Carnden, "New Orleans Photographic Galleries", 245.
44 *Daily Picayune*, September 18, 1859; *Bee*, November 2, 1859.
45 Schleier left New Orleans around 1860 and moved to Nashville, Tennessee, where he practiced his profession through 1866. He was then in Knoxville, Tennessee, in 1872, when he obtained a patent for a photographic camera stand. Nashville city directories, 1860–1866; *Humphrey's Journal*, XVIII (August 15, 1866), 123; Index of patents, 1790– 1873, U.S. Patent Office; *Louisiana Courier*, May 11, 1856. Guay later in 1856 advertised alone, and in 1857 Mealy had his own photographic company. *Courier*, October 17, 1856.

IV

1 *Humphrey's Journal*, XI (April 1, 1860), 355–56.
2 Jenkins, *Images and Enterprise*, 47.
3 Welling, *Photography in America*, 150.
4 Voucher No. 10, July 1859, Acct. 136,399, F. H. Hatch, Agent (Collector of Customs), in Office of First Auditor for Treasury Department, Miscellaneous Treasury Accounts; Thomas K. Wharton to Howell Cobb, Secretary of the Treasury, September 17, 1859, in "Letters Received," Records of Public Buildings Service, Record Group 121; G. T. Beauregard to Howell Cobb, September 7, 1860, in Record Group 121, all in National Archives.
5 Trade card on reverse of photograph of United States Marine Hospital, in Department of Archives and Manuscripts, Troy H. Middleton Library, Louisiana State University.
6 *Daily Picayune*, October 31, 1860; Root, *The Camera and the Pencil*, 303–306.
7 *Gardner's New Orleans Directory*, 1860; Taft, *Photography and the American Scene*, 200.
8 *Daily Picayune*, December 13 and 23, 1859; William Culp Darrah, *The World of Stereographs* (Gettysburg, 1977), 23. Accounts of an exhibition in New Orleans have not yet been located.
9 *Daily Crescent*, November 7, 1859.
10 *Ibid.*, November 4, 1859; Welling, *Photography in America*, 143; *Humphrey's Journal*, XII (February 15, 1861), 305.
11 *Daily Picayune*, March 16 and 25, 1860; Root, *The Camera and the Pencil*, 312; *Humphrey's Journal*, IX (May 1, 1857), 2, VIII (January 1, 1857), 257, VIII (February 15, 1857), 305. The *Photographic and Fine-Art Journal*, XI (August, 1858), 244–45, noted that Law's gallery had the exclusive use of the hallotype in New Orleans. Anderson and Blessing may have purchased the right to make them from Law or been awarded the privilege of making these "improved" hallotypes by Hall himself.

V

1 John D. Winters, *The Civil War in Louisiana* (Baton Rouge, 1963), 21.
2 Charles East to Mary Louise Tucker, January 9, 1980.
3 *Daily Picayune*, May 16, 1861.
4 James Barnes, *The Navies* (New York, 1957), 16–17, Vol. VI of Francis Trevelyan Miller (ed.), *Photographic History of the Civil War*. Print by Edwards with notation of negatives being seized in New Orleans, in Still Pictures Branch, Record Group 77-HL-99-2, National Archives. Information regarding the prints seized from Mallory's home provided by Norman Simons to Mary Louise Tucker, August 13, 1979. New Orleans *Daily Delta*, May 19, 1861; *Daily Picayune*, May 19, 1861; *Daily Delta*, May 16, 1861; *Bee*, May 16, 1861.
5 *Daily Picayune*, April 14, May 12, July 17, 1861. G. P. A. Healy began painting his portrait of General Beauregard in New Orleans but departed with Beauregard and the unfinished painting to South Carolina in the early spring of 1861. His brother, T. C. Healy, made a copy of the partially finished portrait before G. P. A. left the city. This was the portrait Jacobs copied. It was common practice to make photographic copies of paintings of celebrities. These were used in the galleries for display.
6 *Humphrey's Journal*, XII (January 1, 1862), 271; Mr. Van der Weyde to

George Smith Cook, January 19, 1861, in Papers of George Smith Cook, Library of Congress; Welling, *Photography in America*, 169; Taft, *Photography and the American Scene*, 233.

7 *Daily Picayune*, October 8, 1861, April 26, 1862.

8 Winters, *Civil War in Louisiana*, 3–148.

9 *Bee*, December 30, 1862.

10 Andrew Bradford Booth (comp.), *Records of Louisiana Confederate Soldiers and Louisiana Confederate Commands* (New Orleans, 1920), II, 935, for Frobus; Vol. III, Pt. 1, p. 760, for Lilienthals; II, 229, for Camille; II, 419, for Constant; Vol. III, Pt. 1, p. 118, for Guay; Vol. III, Pt. 1, pp. 1071–72, for Moses family. Also see Warren G. Moses to Louisiana State Museum, March 19, 1979.

11 Photograph of "Braddock and John H. Clarke returning from expedition with General Lopez of Mijia's army corp[s] Maximilian's Mexican Foreign Legion, 1865," in the collection of the Louisiana State Museum.

12 *Daily Picayune*, August 26, 1863.

13 Ripley, *Social Life in Old New Orleans*, 126.

14 *Daily Picayune*, September 19, 1863.

15 *Daily Crescent*, November 4, 1859; William B. Welling, *Collectors' Guide to Nineteenth-Century Photographs* (New York, 1976), 31.

16 Joe Gray Taylor, *Louisiana Reconstructed, 1863–1877* (Baton Rouge, 1974), 29–30, 50–52.

17 Winters, *Civil War in Louisiana*, 378.

18 New Orleans *Times-Democrat*, October 16, 1863; *Daily Picayune*, October 16, 1863; *Bee*, September 24, 1863; *L'Abeille de la Nouvelle-Orléans*, May 8, 1863.

19 *Daily Picayune*, September 11, November 1, November 8, 1863.

20 *Ibid.*, February 27, March 13, March 27, 1864.

21 *Trow's New York City Directories*, 1855–56, 1860–61, 1862–63, 1864–65, 1865–66; *Wilson's New York City Co-Partnership Directory*, 1861–62; *Photographic and Fine-Art Journal*, VIII (May, 1855), 160, New Series, III (October, 1856), 320, IV (October, 1857), 320; *Boston City Directory*, 1857–1860; Root, *The Camera and the Pencil*, 382; Welling, *Photography in America*, 113.

22 *Daily Picayune*, November 19, 1864.

23 *Ibid.*, September 2, 1864; *Humphrey's Journal*, XVI (July 15, 1864), 95; (September 1, 1864), 136–37; (October 15, 1864), 181–82.

24 *Daily Picayune*, November 1, 1863, January 19, April 29, 1864.

25 Charles East, *Baton Rouge: A Civil War Album* (Baton Rouge, 1977), 4. Blessing was selling *carte-de-visite* views of the fortifications of Port Hudson in November, 1863. *Daily Picayune*, November 8, 1863.

26 Still Pictures Branch, Record Group 77-F-82-65 through 74 and 74½, for the McPherson and Oliver views; Copyright Records, Louisiana, Eastern District, August 3, 1863, to June, 1870, in Rare Book and Special Collections, Library of Congress.

27 Still Pictures Branch, Record Group 77-F-82-54 through 63, for views of Fort Morgan by Moses and Piffet, dated September 9, 1864.

28 Winters, *Civil War in Louisiana*, 427–28; Shugg, *Origins of Class Struggle*, 194.

VI

1 Winters, *Civil War in Louisiana*, 426

2 Still Pictures Branch, Record Group 165-C-872 to 889. U.S. House of Representatives, 40th Congress, 2nd Session. *Letter from Secretary of War, Transmitting the List of Properties Seized in Louisiana* (Washington, D.C., 1868).

3 Taylor, *Louisiana Reconstructed*, 316, 319.

4 *Ibid.*, 65, 110; *Daily Picayune*, October 12, 1866.

5 Taylor, *Louisiana Reconstructed*, 138; *Gardner's New Orleans Directory*, 1868, p. 9.

6 *Humphrey's Journal*, XVI (July 15, 1864), 95, XVIII (September 15, 1866), 160.

7 *Daily Picayune*, November 20, 1866; *Report of the First Annual Grand Fair of the Mechanics' and Agricultural Fair Association of Louisiana* (New Orleans, 1867), 35.

8 *Daily Picayune*, July 19, 1866.

9 William Culp Darrah, *Stereo Views* (Gettysburg, 1964), 35–39.

10 For instance, several stereo views of Canal Street indicate that Blessing used negatives by W. H. Leeson without acknowledging this fact. W. H. Leeson Collection of Stereo Views, in New Orleans Public Library, and collection of Charles East, Athens, Ga.

11 Lilienthal deposited for copyright twelve photographs representing "Bird's eye views of the City of New Orleans taken from the steeple of St. Patrick Church" on April 13, 1866. Copyright Records, Eastern District, Louisiana, August, 1863, to June, 1870.

12 See reports of the first through the fourth Annual Grand Fairs of the Mechanics' and Agricultural Fair Association of Louisiana, 1867–70; William P. Blake (ed.), *Reports of the United States Commission to the Paris Universal Exposition* (Washington, D.C., 1868), I, 320; Andrew Morrison (ed.), *The Industries of New Orleans* (New Orleans, 1885), 92.

13 *Bee*, August 15, 1865; *Daily Picayune*, August 11, 1865, November 21, 1866; *Report of the First Annual Grand Fair*, 5.

14 *Daily Picayune*, February 26, 1865, July 7, 1866; Succession No. 27,330, Second District Court, Orleans Parish.

15 *Daily Picayune*, October 5, November 10, 1866. On November 8 and 12 Cohen deposited for copyright photos of two actors in their respective roles in *Arrah-Na-Pogue*, an Irish drama that opened at the Varieties Theater on November 5. Copyright Records, Eastern District, Louisiana. *Report of the First Annual Grand Fair*, 5. *Bee*, October 24, 1867.

16 *Report of the First Annual Grand Fair*, 5; *Report of the Second Annual Grand Fair*, 2; *Daily Picayune*, November 16, 1903.

17 Warren G. Moses to the Louisiana State Museum, March 19, 1979.

18 *Report of the Second Annual Grand Fair*, 1, 4; John Dobran, "The Spirits of Mumler," *Northlight*, Vol. V, Pt. 1 (Spring, 1978), 4–7, Vol. V, Pt. 2 (Summer, 1978), 10–14.

19 Franklin M. Garrett, Atlanta Historical Society, February 27, 1980; *Weatherbe's Atlanta, Georgia Duplex City Directory, 1886*; *The Directory of Atlanta, Georgia, 1887* (Norwood, Connelly & Co.); *Atlanta City Directory for 1888*.

20 Orleans Parish. Second District Court. Succession Records No. 29,768.

21 *Ibid.*, No. 29,817. Andrew Bradford Booth (comp.), *Records of Louisiana Confederate Soldiers* (New Orleans, 1920), Vol. III, Book 2, p. 206.

22 Trade card, in a collection of Leeson stereographs, New Orleans Public Library.

23 *L'Abeille de la Nouvelle-Orléans*, April 1, May 11, 1865.

24 Welling, *Photography in America*, 185.

25 *Ibid.*

Bibliography

Published Materials

BOOKS

Blake, William P., ed. *Reports of the United States Commission to the Paris Universal Exposition, 1867*. Vol. I. Washington, D.C.: Government Printing Office, 1870.

Booth, Andrew Bradford, comp. *Records of Louisiana Confederate Soldiers and Louisiana Confederate Commands*. New Orleans: n. p., 1920.

Burgess, Nathan G. *The Photograph Manual: A Practical Treatise . . . Various Alkaline Toning Baths, etc. etc.* Literature of Photography. New York: Arno Press, 1973. Originally published in 1863.

Castle, Peter. *Collecting and Valuing Old Photographs*. London: Garnstone Press, 1973.

Chute, William Joseph. *Damn Yankee! The First Career of Frederick A. P. Barnard, Educator, Scientist, Idealist*. Port Washington, N.Y.: Kennikat Press, 1978.

Cirker, Hayward, and Blanche Cirker. *Dictionary of American Portraits*. New York: Dover Publications, 1967.

Darrah, William Culp. *Stereo Views*. Gettysburg: Time & News, 1964.

———. *The World of Stereographs*. Gettysburg: n.p., 1977.

Davis, Edwin A. *Louisiana: A Narrative History*. Baton Rouge: Claitor's Publishing Division, 1971.

Dunlap, William. *Diary of William Dunlap*. Vol. III. New York: n.p., 1830.

East, Charles. *Baton Rouge: A Civil War Album*. Baton Rouge: n.p., 1977.

Eder, Josef Maria. *History of Photography*. Translated by Edward Epstean. New York: Dover, 1978. Originally published in 1945.

Fielding, Mantle. *Dictionary of American Painters, Sculptors, and Engravers*. New York: James F. Carr, 1965.

Gernsheim, Helmut, and Alison Gernsheim. *The History of Photography: From the Camera Obscura to the Beginning of the Modern Era*. New York: McGraw Hill, 1969.

———. *L. J. M. Daguerre: The History of the Diorama and the Daguerreotype*. Rev. ed. New York: Dover, 1968.

Groce, George C., and David H. Wallace. *The New-York Historical Society's Dictionary of Artists in America, 1564–1860*. New Haven: Yale University Press, 1957.

Hall, A. Oakey. *The Manhattaner in New Orleans: Or, Phases of Crescent City Life*. Baton Rouge: Louisiana State University Press, 1976. Originally published in 1851.

Herring, James, and J. B. Longacre, eds. *National Portrait Gallery of Distinguished Americans, with Biographical Sketches*. Vol. II. Philadelphia: Rice and Hart, 1854.

Industries of Houston. Houston: J. M. Elstner, 1887.

Janson, Horst W., comp. *Catalogues of the Paris Salon, 1673 to 1881*. New York: Garland Publications, 1977.

Jenkins, Reese V. *Images and Enterprise*. Baltimore: Johns Hopkins University Press, 1975.

Kocher, A. Lawrence, and Howard Dearstyne. *Shadows in Silver: A Record of Virginia, 1850–1900, in Contemporary Photographs Taken by George and Huestis Cook*. New York: Charles Scribner's Sons, 1954.

Miller, Francis Trevelyan, ed. *Photographic History of the Civil War*. New York: T. Yoseloff, 1957.

Morrison, Andrew, ed. *The Industries of New Orleans*. New Orleans: J. M. Elstner, 1885.

New Orleans As It Is, by a Resident. New Orleans [?]: n.p., 1850.

Newhall, Beaumont. *The Daguerreotype in America*. 3rd rev. ed. New York: Dover, 1976.

———. *The History of Photography*. 4th ed. New York: Museum of Modern Art, 1964.

Perry, Regina A. *Selections of 19th Century Afro-American Art*. New York: Metropolitan Museum of Art, 1976.

Reilly, James M. *The Albumen and Salted Paper Book: The History and Practice of Photographic Printing, 1840–1895*. Rochester: Light Impressions, 1980.

Reinders, Robert C. *End of an Era: New Orleans 1850–1860*. New Orleans: Pelican, 1964.

Report of the First Annual Grand Fair of the Mechanics' and Agricultural Fair Association of Louisiana. New Orleans: n.p., 1867.

Report of the Second Annual Grand Fair of the Mechanics' and Agricultural Fair Association of Louisiana. New Orleans: n.p., 1868.

Report of the Third Annual Grand Fair of the Mechanics' and Agricultural Fair Association of Louisiana. New Orleans: n.p., 1869.

Report of the Fourth Annual Grand Fair of the Mechanics' and Agricultural Fair Association of Louisiana. New Orleans: n.p., 1870.

Rinhart, Floyd, and Marion Rinhart. *American Daguerreian Art.* New York: Clarkson N. Potter, 1967.

Ripley, Eliza. *Social Life in Old New Orleans: Being Recollections of My Girlhood.* New York: D. Appleton, 1912.

Root, Marcus A. *The Camera and the Pencil, or the Heliographic Art.* Philadelphia: M. A. Root, J. B. Lippincott, 1864; rpr. Pawlet, Vt.: Helios Press, 1971.

Rudisill, Richard. *Mirror Image: The Influence of the Daguerreotype on American Society.* Albuquerque: University of New Mexico Press, 1971.

Saunders, James Edmonds. *Early Settlers of Alabama.* New Orleans: L. Graham & Son, 1899.

Siegel, Martin, ed. *New Orleans: A Chronological and Documentary History, 1539–1970.* Dobbs Ferry: Oceana, 1975.

Shugg, Roger W. *Origins of Class Struggle in Louisiana: A Social History of White Farmers and Laborers During Slavery and After, 1840–1875.* Baton Rouge: Louisiana State University Press, 1939.

Simons, Montgomery P. *Plain Instructions for Colouring Photographs in Water Colours and India Ink.* Philadelphia: T. K. and P. G. Collins, 1857.

Soulé, Leon Cyprian. *The Know-Nothing Party in New Orleans: A Reappraisal.* Baton Rouge: n.p., 1961.

Taft, Robert. *Photography and the American Scene: A Social History, 1839–1889.* New York: Dover, 1964. Originally published in 1938.

Taylor, Joe Gray. *Louisiana Reconstructed, 1863–1877.* Baton Rouge: Louisiana State University Press, 1975.

U.S. House of Representatives, 40th Cong., 2nd Sess. *Letter from Secretary of War, Transmitting the List of Properties Seized in Louisiana.* Washington, D.C.: Government Printing Office, 1868.

Welling, William. *Collectors' Guide to Nineteenth-Century Photographs.* New York: Collier Books, 1976.

———. *Photography in America: The Formative Years, 1839–1900.* New York: Thomas Y. Crowell, 1978.

Winters, John D. *The Civil War in Louisiana.* Baton Rouge: Louisiana State University Press, 1963.

Young, William. *A Dictionary of American Artists, Sculptors, and Engravers.* Cambridge, Mass.: William Young, 1968.

PERIODICALS

Affleck's Southern Rural Almanac (1851).
Anthony's Photographic Bulletin, XVI (February 14, 1885).
Ballou's Dollar Monthly Magazine, II (December, 1855).
Barnard, F. A. P. "Improvement in the Daguerreotype Process of Photography." *American Journal of Science and Arts*, XLI (October, 1841), 352–54.
Bogardus, Abraham. "The Lost Art of the Daguerreotype." *Century Magazine*, LXVIII (May, 1904), 83–91.
Busey, Samuel C. "Early History of Daguerreotypy in the City of Washington." *Records of the Columbia Historical Society*, III (1900), 93–95.
Carnden, R. A. "New Orleans Photographic Galleries." *Photography and Fine-Art Journal*, XI (August, 1858), 244–45.
Cohen, A. D. "George S. Cook and the Daguerrean Art," *Photographic Art-Journal*, I (May, 1851), 285–87.
DaguerreianJournal (1850–1851).
Dobran, John. "The Spirits of Mumler." *Northlight*, Vol. V. Pt. 1 (Spring, 1978), 4–7; Vol. V, Pt. 2 (Summer, 1978), 10–14.
Humphrey's Journal, Devoted to the Daguerreian and Photogenic Arts (1852–1862).
Humphrey's Journal of Photography, Chemistry, and Pharmacy (1862–1863).
Humphrey's Journal of Photography and the Heliographic Arts and Sciences (1863).
Humphrey's Journal of Photography and the Allied Arts and Sciences (1863–1870).
Niles' Weekly Register. LXIII (February 11, 1843).
"Photogenic Drawing." *United States Magazine and Democratic Review*, V (May, 1839), 517–20.
Photographic Art-Journal. (1851–53).
Photographic and Fine-Art Journal (1854–60).

NEWSPAPERS

L'Abeille de la Nouvelle-Orléans
New Orleans *Bee*
New Orleans *Commercial Bulletin*
New Orleans *Commercial Times*
Le Courrier de la Louisiane
New Orleans *Daily Crescent*
New Orleans *Daily Delta*
Baton Rouge *Daily Gazette and Comet*
New Orleans *Daily Orleanian*

New Orleans *Daily Picayune*
New Orleans *Daily Tropic*
New Orleans *Daily True Delta*
Nashville *Daily Union*
Baton Rouge *Gazette*
Gazette de Baton Rouge
Louisiana Courier
Louisiana Spectator
Louisiana State Republican
New Orleans *New Delta*
New Orleans *Semi-Weekly Creole*
Lafayette *Southern Traveler*
Port Allen *Sugar Planter*
New Orleans *Times-Democrat*
Baton Rouge Weekly Gazette and Comet

CITY DIRECTORIES

Atlanta City Directory, 1888 through 1900
Boston City Directory, 1857 through 1860
Cohen's New Orleans and Lafayette Directory, 1849 through 1852
Cohen's New Orleans Directory, 1853 through 1855
Cohen's New Orleans and Southern Directory, 1856
Concord [N.H.] *Directory*, 1856
Crescent City Business Directory, 1858–59
Directory of Atlanta, Georgia, 1886, 1887
Doggett's New York City Directory, 1842–43, 1846–47
Edward's New Orleans Directory,1870
Edward's Business Directory for Louisiana and Mississippi, 1870 and 1871
Gardner's and Wharton's New Orleans Directory, 1858
Gardner's New Orleans Business Directory, 1866
Gardner's New Orleans Directory, 1859 through 1861, 1866 through 1869
Gibson's Guide and Directory of the State of Louisiana and the Cities of Lafayette and New Orleans, 1838
Graham's New Orleans Directory, 1867
Graham's Crescent City Directory, 1870
King's Nashville Directory, 1866
Longworth's American Almanac, New York Register, and City Directory, 1842
Merrill & Son's Concord [N.H.] *City Directory*, 1860–61
Michel & Co. New Orleans Annual and Commercial Register, 1846
Mygatt's New Orleans Directory, 1857
Nashville City and Business Directory, 1860–61

New Orleans Merchant's Diary and Guide, 1857 and 1858
New Orleans Pictorial Advertiser, 1849
New York City Directory, 1845 and 1846
New York Mercantile Register, 1847–48, 1848–49, 1849–50
Normand's New Orleans Business Directory, 1845 and 1846
Pitts & Clarke's Guide and Directory: New Orleans, Lafayette, Algiers & Gretna, 1842
Sheldon and Co.'s Business or Advertising Directory, 1845
Singleton's Nashville Business Directory, 1865
Ten Eyck's Washington and Georgetown Directory, 1855
Trow's New York City Directory, 1855–56, 1860–61, 1862–63, 1863–64, 1864–65, 1865–66
Washington and Georgetown Directory, 1853
Weatherbe's Atlanta, Georgia, Duplex City Directory, 1886
Wilson's New York City Co-Partnership Directory, 1861–62

Unpublished Materials

MANUSCRIPTS

Library of Congress, Washington, D.C.

Manuscript Division
Cook, George Smith. Papers, 1845–1861.
Morse, Samuel F. B. Papers.
Rare Book and Special Collections
Copyright Records. Louisiana, Eastern District. August, 1863, to June, 1870.

Louisiana State Museum Library, New Orleans
Artists of New Orleans and Their Pictures. Scrapbook.
Tombstone Inscriptions of New Orleans Cemeteries. Card File.

Troy H. Middleton Library, Louisiana State University, Baton Rouge
Department of Archives and Manuscripts
Duncan, Herman Cope, and Family. Papers.
Dunham, Marshall R. Album.
Solomon, Clara E. Diary, 1861–62.

National Archives, Washington, D.C.
Records of Public Buildings Service. Record Group 121.
Still Pictures Branch. Record Group 77–F–82–65–74 and 74½, 77–F–82–54–63, 77–HL–99–2, 165–C–872–889.
Miscellaneous Treasury Accounts. Office of First Auditor for Treasury Department.

New Orleans Public Library
Index to Obituaries in New Orleans Newspapers. Card File.
Leeson, W. H. Collection of Stereo Views.
New Orleans Census Records for 1850, 1860, 1870 [microfilm].
Orleans Parish. Index of Death Certificates. Vol. 161 [microfilm].
Orleans Parish. Second District Court Succession Records, Fourth District Court Succession Records [microfilm].

Tangipahoa Parish Courthouse, Amite, La.
Records of Conveyance.

U.S. Patent Office, Washington, D.C.
Index of Patents, 1790–1873.

Valentine Museum, Richmond, Va.
Cook, George S. Papers.

THESIS

Thompson, N. Ruth Farr. "A Biographical Checklist of Artists in New Orleans in the 19th Century." M.A. thesis, Louisiana State University, 1970.

CORRESPONDENCE

Battle, Martha E., North Carolina Museum of History, Raleigh, N.C., to Mary Louise Tucker, August 15, 1979.
East, Charles, to authors, January 9 and May 27, 1980.
Garrett, Franklin M., Atlanta Historical Society, to authors, February 27, 1980.
Haynes, David, Institute of Texas Cultures, University of Texas at San Antonio, to Mary Louise Tucker, April 17 and August 28, 1978.
Moses, Warren G., to Louisiana State Museum, March 19, 1979.
Nygren, Deborah, W. S. Hoole Special Collections, University of Alabama, to authors, September 1, 1978.
Simon, Norman, Pensacola Historical Museum, Florida, to Mary Louise Tucker, August 3, 1979.

Index